The Drive-thru Museum

A journey across the everyday USA

Andy Soutter

i
impact books

For Rosey, and all our hosts

Acknowledgements:
The quotation on p. vi from *The Western Lands* © 1987 by
William S. Burroughs is reprinted with the permission of
Wylie, Aitken & Stone, Inc.

Front and Back cover photographs were taken by the
author.

First published in Great Britain 1993
by Impact Books, 112 Bolingbroke Grove,
London SW11 1DA

ISBN 1-874687-09-9

Typeset by
Roger King Graphic Studios, Poole, Dorset.

Printed and bound by The Guernsey Press, Guernsey

Contents

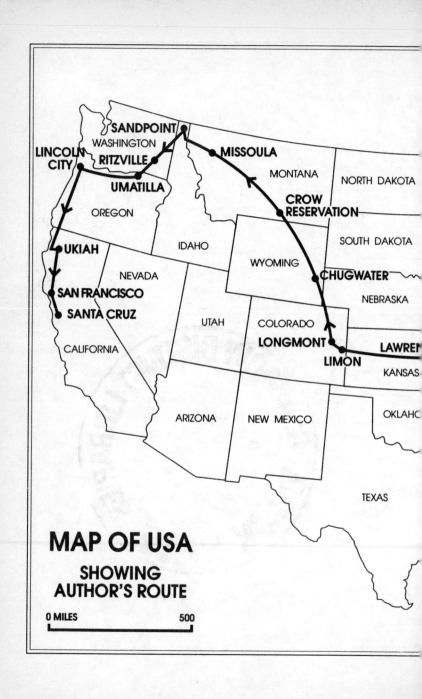

MAP OF USA

SHOWING
AUTHOR'S ROUTE

0 MILES   500

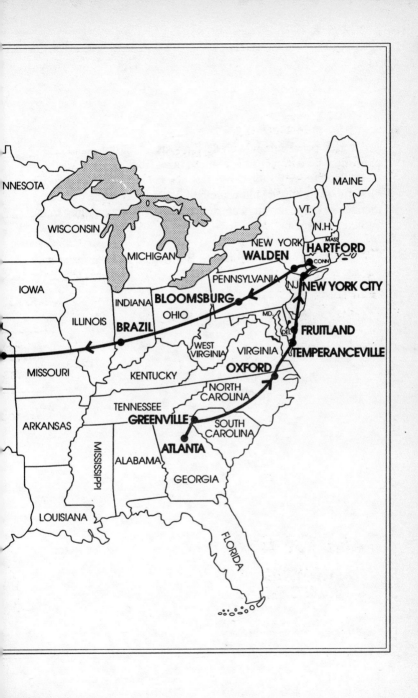

A deserted penal colony with dead ghosts . . . pasture land opposite where implausible ponies graze. Does anyone ride them? Do they pull little carts? Do they lay back their ears and bite with their horrid yellow teeth? I doubt it . . . a line of trees, then white grain elevators crash into the sky like a painting in the Whitney Museum.

William S. Burroughs, *The Western Lands*

PREFACE

A Nation in Menopause?

I can date the change from a day in 1960 when there appeared in the windows of John Barnes department store at Swiss Cottage, London a remarkable display. At that time my world was as American as anywhere in urban Europe. Apart from the hybrids on my block – a Filipino kid called Delano; a couple of brothers of an Anglo-Yank marriage named Shane and Earl; and the cars of Anglo-Yank heritage, notably the garish Vauxhall Crestas and Victors – there were the real Americans: most obviously a brand-new pale blue Chevrolet Impala convertible which was parked next door on the street, outrageously long and wide, with twinned headlamps and a rear end sculpted like albatross wings. I was spellbound when this beauty first appeared, doubly ecstatic shortly afterwards when I was able to buy a Corgi-toy version of it – and then, to top if off, I even got a lift to school in it sometimes along with Micky, the son of its owners. It was so smooth and silent I couldn't believe the engine was on, and 'lift' was the right word – I floated to school those mornings. Micky it was, too, who sometimes nicked his folks' imported cigarettes, also long and smooth: they were called Viceroy. Something of a hint of colonial administration here.

But the Americans in our neighbourhood were mostly in show business. There was more than one family with a rugged, chiselled father whose job it was to play the token Yank in the British films of the day. Every homegrown movie seemed to have one, no matter how implausible the role might be, because this was supposed to be the only way to flog the flick on the other side of the pond, as well as imbuing it with extra glamour for the home market: thus dramas set in the wilds of Northumberland or amongst the kitchen sinks of Leeds would always have some lone, incongruous, well-groomed American of unlikely or unexplained background to save the heroine in the last reel and be warmly thanked by the local baggy-suited RADA-voiced police superintendent: '... and if you're ever in Melchester again, Mr Glendale ...' Even such apparently indigenous product as the long-running *Robin Hood* kids' series on TV had America to thank for its success: it was scripted by an expat American who had been blackballed in his own country during the McCarthy era ... and its star, Richard Greene, had more than a touch of Stewart Grainger about him.

But there was plenty of genuine Americana for my delectation: comics like *Spooky (tuff little ghost), Archie, Superman,* and the rest, their ad sections full of strange talk of Zip Codes and Marches of Dimes. And at Saturday morning pictures, *Tom & Jerry*, *Bugs Bunny*, Roy Rogers, and *The Cisco Kid*; and on the airwaves and in the pegboarded listening booths at W H Smiths there was Elvis, Bobby Vee, Pat Boone and all their British imitators. At breakfast time my older sister would play the *West Side Story* soundtrack while I munched on cereal courtesy of Nabisco or General Foods; at school the boys would trade Rastus-and-Liza jokes – which dwelt on the supposed hypersexuality of black Americans – along with imported American tit magazines, which were the first examples of pornography ever to get my little stem twitching; while the girls wore pony tails and played with hula-hoops; and in the evening my father might come home with a Penguin Charles Addams or a collection of Whitney Darrow Jr cartoons, or Jules Ffeiffer sketches (he who was already taking the piss out of modern dancers and neurotic Yanks in the pages of the Sunday *Observer)*, or a copy of *Evergreen Review* (poems by Ginsberg, articles about Olson). Everyone was looking to the USA: to entertain, to save us from the Russians, and to save us from drudgery with their standards of domestic technology – the big fridges, the washing machines, the self-changing record players ... and what was that thing they pointed at their (enormous) TVs which miraculously changed the channel?

And then came that John Barnes window display. At first you might have thought the windows were empty; but all along the long, wide frontage, arranged on low shelves near the front of the glass, was a collection of small maroon rectangular leather-clad objects. John Barnes' displays were always discreet, so there were no eye-catching flyers. You had to go right up close to read the modestly printed card next to the little leather briquettes. The card read: 'Transistor Radios. Made in Japan. £12.'

Things were never the same after that. It wasn't an object's size that mattered, it was what you did with it. Suddenly the world was in love with little things – little radios, little skirts, little cars, small-wheeled foldaway bikes, Honda 50s, tape-cassettes: and it was Europe and Japan doing all the inventing. A Japanese kid showed up at school; his name (as I spelled it in my head) was York Macassar, and he was a happy little kid who was always running everywhere, very fast. For all I know his dad was sales manager for Sanyo. Soon the Nipponese trannies would be followed by 'tapecorders' and motorbikes. England would watch all-British films on Sony TVs and re-export rock'n'roll back to the States. London would swing: Mini cars, mini-cabs and *The Avengers*. The only American actor left in town would be Vincent Price, an ageing ghost.

And America itself was about to break out in hot flushes. By 1960 it had long ago given birth to, then suckled and raised the modern world. It wasn't a young country anymore. From now on its creativity might have to be of a different order.

It was in this same year that my mother's periods stopped. I remember six or seven years of anger, confusion, insecurity and neuralgias before she resettled herself and found confidence in her future. But America is not a woman, even though with a latitudinal stretch of the imagination it does resemble a gigantic womb. Its own midlife crisis has lasted much longer: thirty years of prostate trouble. Throughout this time its only second coming (to mangle Yeats) has been as its best are convicted and its worst are filled with passionate density.

Going into space did seem like a creative act, but the project deteriorated. It became more a matter of pride and honour than of curiosity – a mere race with the then Soviet Union, just another Olympic Games, another orgy of speed, distance, mensuration, tabulation, spiritless abstraction. And not even any blacks to stand on the moon and raise their fists like they had done from the winners' podium in Mexico City.

Thirty years of turmoil, race riots, bloody murders and self-analyses were to follow, thirty years of unresolved arguments about God, War, Abortion, Racism, Narcotics, Women, Guns, Taxes. Meanwhile the basic technologies have remained the same, the last ageing-president-who-saw-service-in-World-War-Two has only just departed, and in the nineties they have been rioting nationwide for the same reasons they did in 1965. As far as the US is concerned, the past is very definitely not another country, not even another town – it's right there on everybody's doorstep.

In 1960 I wasn't to visit the USA for almost another three decades; but when I did make it, I had the feeling that it had put itself on hold until I could finally show up. It was a foreign place, but a familiar place. I found much of my own past right there in this other country. It had been well buried in my own: Europe's struggle over the last fifty years has been to re-invent itself, while America's has been one of preservation.

Three years after that first trip in 1988, I returned. In August and September 1991, my companion and I bought an old Japanese car and drove across the continent, from Georgia in the South to New York and Connecticut and thence through the Midwest and up to the northern Rockies before ending our journey in California. We stayed in numerous motels and imposed upon seven households.

America used to be the place where the future happened first; but wherever we went I found a nation hooked on its past, from its movies and TV to the question of who killed JFK, from Freudian therapeutic strategies to an obsession with the morals and deeds of the ancient Israelites. In everyday American landscapes, domestic trappings, and in the way people move, speak and dress, the past is invoked to an extraordinary degree, while the future seems to be on ice for the duration. So many Americans are worried about their jobs and their country's newly reduced economic status; they distrust their institutions; they are looking back – for someone to blame or else for something familiar to comfort them.

All this made for a journey strewn with anachronisms, through a country whose past is so much more visible in every building and attitude than is the case in Britain, whose own history tends to be ghetto-ized in the realm of the spectacular (the medieval castles, the grand events of state). But America's yesterdays are

locked into its everyday life, clearly visible in the most ordinary
architectures and mundane actions. Thus we drove through an
extraordinary coast-to-coast exhibition of a country beset by relics
and looking back in earnest to Elvis, Jesus, the fifties, its parents,
its martyrs, its automobiles, its jobs. A country smelling of
cinnamon, where trees and ducks were brightly ribboned, where
seventeenth-century German peasants ate Big Macs and
milkshakes, and where we were always likely to discover Calvary
around the next bend.

I also found a peculiar foreignness – such as would only affect
a Britisher. To put it simply: what makes Americans so weird is
the fact that they speak English. This raises certain expectations in
a British visitor, who will presume that because the tongue is
familiar, so therefore will be the concurrent attitudes and
behaviour patterns. It is when these expectations are not met that
all of America's bizarrities – sinister, admirable, outrageous or just
plain cute – seem doubly strange, doubly repellent or doubly
attractive, depending on your point of view. Travelling through
America's heartlands, I found myself in a country dominated by
Saxons. The Anglo influence has long been just a vestige. And if
logic ruled this earth, the official language of the USA would be
German: for this has been its dominant cultural influence for more
than a century (in fact some people claim that the very foundations
of the American state are based on the doctrines of a group of
Bavarian Freemasons). However, logic's loss has been this
writer's gain. To be a stranger in a strange land is always
stimulating; but to be a stranger in a familiar land has a flavour all
of its own: the sublime taste of paradox.

1. The Murdered Princess

There was enough tarmac here to pave the entire interstate system and we were taking an age to cross it. I fiddled impatiently with a sweaty plastic domino. Then I remembered you have to slow down when coming to the USA. It's not a fast country, not at all. It does have its moments of convulsive activity, but between times like any large beast it is ponderous and patient. Republicans ride an elephant; democrats ride a mule. They spend much of their lives sitting – on porches, in pews, in courtrooms, in cars. Slow, slow, slow. Slow as this heavy reptile was lumbering us past endless ranks of parked aircraft glistening silver in the sunlight, wave upon wave of them. Slow as a sea crossing. Slow as the Civil War. Slow as the conquest of the West. Slow as an atom bomb. Slow as Elvis. Momentously slow. Slow as shopping for groceries in a mile-wide Winn-Dixie. Slow as this DC10 of ours wandering up and down the runways of Atlanta airport like a lost trolley looking for the checkout. So much space, so much time.

We had a date with another aircraft, two months from now in San Francisco. Between now and then we aimed to cross the country by car, starting here in the South and then backtracking up to New York and Connecticut before heading west. It worked out at about six thousand miles in sixty days – a leisurely one hundred miles per day average. We had a dog-eared Rand McNally and a piece of shoestring disguised as a credit card.

My wallet also contained a photograph of a loved one. It was a long, low-slung 1973 Dodge Dart sedan, an elegant creature which I'd bought three years before for a trip around the South. Built in the last year before OPEC finally drew a line underneath the post-war economic order, it was already an antique – a gas-eater, the sort of wreck that only blacks or wizzened old white men drove these days. But I loved it dearly. For a start it cost a mere three hundred dollars. On top of that its seats put the furniture in my London flat to shame; it cornered like a ship; it was reliable – one of Detroit's flukier models that came along every once in a while – and it had automatic transmission, which meant I could drive with one foot tucked up on the seat (good for my back pain) and one arm free to hang out of the window (good for my image). Basically, though, it was big. And I had been used to hustling around in London traffic cramped fit to suffocate and working a stick shift till my wrists ached like those of a ten-year-old who has just discovered another kind of stick with infinitely more joy attached to it. I had loved my Dodge so much that I had not sold it on leaving, and now I looked forward to continuing the affair.

I had loved America, too, for all sorts of reasons, but what had intrigued me most was a mysterious emotional response: the feeling that I was coming home. I was feeling it again now, and I couldn't explain it. I was aware that I'd grown up like so many others in the grip of the US's cultural hegemony. I knew exactly where I was when I first heard Elvis (curled up under the blankets, headphoned, listening to Radio Luxembourg on my crystal set); when JFK was shot (staring into the aghast face of my history teacher, shocked at *his* shock); when the astronauts first danced on the moon (at a friend's house learning the chords to a Robert Johnson blues); and when Elvis died (curled up on a sofa, headphoned, listening to Miles Davis). And as a student of contemporary arts I was taught by Americans and I studied Americans; so this was the land of my mentors – but knowing all this had not dispelled the mystery of that intriguing voltage between gut and brain I felt when standing on hard American soil, breathing sharp American air, and witnessing that vast American light which seems to have more photons per cubic inch than anywhere else in the world, and which was already flooding this aircraft cabin with an extra dimension. So there was unfinished business.

Eventually we were disgorged at the terminal. At passport control a Slim Pickens wannabe lounged back in his chair and flipped idly through my passport. 'So you're a writer, huh?' he said, real slow, real poker-faced.

'That's right,' I said.

He looked up slowly and fixed me with a stare. 'You a *good* one?' he said, as if it was a qualification for entry. I offered him a copy of my book, but he waved me through, dead-pan.

The other side of customs we found Richard waiting for us. He welcomed us to America in an impeccable middle-class English voice. Richard can do all kinds of accents, but this was the one he was born with. His surname is Ffarington, and I never know which f is silent. Or why there are two in the first place; perhaps one of his forebears stuttered in front of the census-taker. Richard doesn't stutter – his diction is always clear. He's a man of the theatre, after all. So we have to hug. It's just something you have to do. But I admire the stiffness and reserve of Richard's hug – it's one which definitely does not recall crush bars infested with dancerly dahlings. In fact it militates against all that. Hugging Richard, I feel his hard mortal bones, his reality and his resistance.

He leads us out to the car park in his old black shirt, tatty trousers and a pair of oversize red running shoes; marching briskly, arms a-swing, feet asplay, a gait inherited from the OTC of his schooldays. Our company halts beside an old blue Toyota, now fast turning yellow as the sun burns through to the undercoat. While Rosey admires a stretch limo parked next to us, I admire the heavy, clinging heat – the embrace of the South. Better than any massage. However, the Toyota is air-conditioned. I'll have to bear it. Ahead of us is a three-hour ride north-east along Interstate 85 to the Carolina line.

President Dwight D. Eisenhower is the man they credit with initiating the interstate highway system back in the late 1950s; indeed they've named a lot of stretches after him. It seems appropriate enough that a wartime general who had seen service in Europe and appreciated the benefits – civil and military – that Germany's autobahns bestowed upon that country should want to import them to his own. The president's name alone, reeking of blood and iron and Bismarckian heroics, appears to have ensured success for the project, and in less than thirty years the network is more or less complete. The result isn't particularly romantic. It has not been enshrined in oils like the old highways – Hopper's *Gas Station*, for example: the tall pumps with the two-lane blacktop plunging away into a dark Dantean forest. It has not been celebrated much in road movies, which tend to stick with highways. There are songs such as 'Route 66', but as yet no

'I-95'; and there have been no native Americans with names like Least Heat Moon to wax lyrical about these giant dual carriageways with their attendant truck weigh stations, landscaped rest-and-picnic areas and fast-food plazas. Not yet, anyway. It's only a matter of time. One day, when everything is teletransported or whatever, people will take relatively slow, sentimental journeys along these arteries, and they will commune with the ghosts of a past age, in the same way as people today take leisurely trips along Britain's ancient canals, and admire all that industrial archaeology: the quaint typographies, the weeds in the cracks. But for now, modern America rides around on this German invention. Proposed, invented and constructed first during the Hitler days. You could even say, Nazi invention.

There's a great deal of Germany evident in contemporary America, not least its trunk road system, and plenty of this smacks of the pre-war period. Previously, in the South, I had seen gas stations called Hess, and truck trailers bearing the name Heil; and Richard Ffarington had pointed out to me with his suspicious-yet-excited sense of awe, the prevalent typography of the land: in letterheads, public notices and commercial signs, neon-lit names of motels and drugstores and supermarkets – the curvaceous lettering, slim, the tops of capital letters rounded, and letters like M and N resembling the lower case.

'Remind you of anything?' he had said. Yes, Bauhaus.

'Reminds me of the decade after,' said Richard.

That had been three years ago. Right now we were racing along Atlanta's expressways and catching up with each other's news. We stopped for gas and junk food, and inside the shop a balding old gentleman was being required to show ID proving he was over twenty-one and allowed to buy beer. 'Sorry, sir, it's the rules.'

'I'm flattered. I got a grandson who's twenty-two.'

Yes, we were in the South. Where people say *doggone it* and have an uncomfortable relationship with alcohol.

This part of north Georgia has a pretty undistinguished landscape, which is just as well because you don't get to see much of it from the road, which is lined with tall, impenetrable pines hung about thickly with kudzu vine. Kudzu was originally a Japanese import and appeared around the turn of the century, acquired for the horticultural glories of its large white flowers;

subsequently its proliferate nature and ability to suck the life out of any tree it entwined were used to prevent the encroachment of woodland on to highway; but after this it became a notorious nuisance to anyone working the land since it spreads so rapidly and embeds itself so tenaciously in the soil. What was at first pretty, and then useful, finally became strangulatory. Kudzu may well have coloured more than one American's attitude towards Japan.

The beige concrete of the interstate stretches ahead with barely a curve in vast, gentle undulations, and half an hour out of Atlanta there's very little traffic. Trucks passing in the opposite direction seem uncannily distant because of the immense stretch of wooded median which separates the carriageways: we see their devil's-horn exhaust pipes poking up each side of the cab, puffing black smoke. We overtake the odd pick-up; the odd pick-up overtakes us. It's a quiet, forlorn route through an underpopulated part of the land – the soil is poor, the towns few and far between; moreover they remain unseen. So far America is revealing little of itself except its scale. We can see the sign for 'Fuel City' high in the sky like a distant yellow moon for miles before we reach it, jacked up on its telescopic pole above a truck stop up on the embankment where a highway arches over our route. Here in the gas station shop with its small café, America reveals its coffee – bottomless and flavourless. A sip of things to come. We gulp down our feeble percolations and leave. Before too long, with darkness falling, we quit the interstate at the sign for Westminster, where South Carolina Welcomes Us. We take Highway 11, a narrow blacktop winding northwards past scattered smatterings of cheap homesteads with clutches of old cars out front and the stars and stripes hanging limp from a pole or a porch. While inside the Toyota the Welsh Dragon hangs from the dashboard.

Richard hates being an Englishman. He's been denying it most of his life. He didn't like the conservatism of his parents or his private school in Herefordshire, so he kicked against the pricks until he crossed the border and went to college in Newport and made a Welshman of himself – gregarious, passionate, and ever-mindful of English tyranny. Nevertheless he eventually migrated to London, and after this he made theatre in the wacky world of seventies' Amsterdam. For a while he lived with a woman in

Memphis, Tennessee, but he came back to work in London in 1979, just as the queen of a new political order was taking her throne. Bad timing for someone whose work depended on public money. He took it personally. He has always called her 'She', through gritted teeth, as if Thatcher were a vindictive aunt living permanently in his front room. And to anyone he meets, he says he's Welsh. He doesn't want any connection with that strand of Englishness to which he has felt unfortunately attached since birth – an irritating umbilical cord which, since he can't sever it, he has hung with Welsh flags. He met his American wife in a love-at-first-sight encounter on the bridge at Camden Lock in 1985, and although he still keeps a flat in London, he spends more and more time based in South Carolina, where he acts and directs and teaches and does TV and film parts cast for true-blue limeys. He'll be an American citizen soon, but I can't see him ever flying the stars and stripes.

An hour along the deserted Highway 11, through forest, across lake, past small townships, with mountains looming in the dark to our left, we turn on to a gritty side road and drive for a mile or so through the pines before turning into a break in the trees. Here we cross some perilously rickety planks that bridge a small creek and then lurch up a short rutted dirt track before coming to a halt. In front of us is a traditional old two-roomed southern shack: squatting on stone piles, timber-sided, rusted tin roof, crooked chimney and mythic porch. Facing this shack, all lit up and a good deal less romantic, is a long rectangular trailer home. A woman with a mass of thick brown hair, T-shirt and shorts, is sliding open the screen door. She beams at us and says 'Hi y'all!' in a country-pure soprano.

This is Judy, and her father owns this and all the land hereabouts. Most of it is pine forest, and there's some pasture he rents out to a farmer. He and his wife live a half-mile up the road. Richard and Judy also stayed there till recently while they renovated the old shack, which they had planned to live in. It stands in a three-acre clearing which in 1986 was three acres of solid scrap metal. It took them two years of work just to clear the clearing of old automobiles, bedsteads, fridges and every kind of tangled rusted horror imaginable. The shack's interior also was piled high with junk, the walls were covered in thick brown smoke tar and the place had no amenities or running water. The grease monkey who had resided there till his death had lived in just those conditions – it wasn't that anything had accumulated since. Richard and Judy gave every hour they could spare to the place. They cleared the shack, painted up the rooms, raked the soil over and over to rid it of deeply embedded ferric trash, communing with scorpions, lizards and turtles as they went, cleared the kudzu, ploughed the earth, planted a vegetable patch, hooked up telephone and electricity, dammed a spring back up in the woods and piped water down from it, and finally – didn't move in. Earlier this year they found a snip of a sixty-foot trailer home for five hundred bucks, decided its fitted kitchen and carpets, two bedrooms, two bathrooms and lounge would be far more comfortable, and had it delivered and set opposite the shack, which is now a workshop and pottery studio for Judy. Their only regret is that a week after moving into the trailer a film location crew showed up and just loved the shack – so funky, so period – and would have paid them plenty more than $500 to shoot there if it wasn't for the newly installed mohome. 'Ho, hum,' says Richard.

They didn't clear the land entirely of junk. In one corner a rusting Rambler stationwagon glares with twinned headlamps. Obsolete Pepsi crates have been preserved. Obscure metal artifacts are stacked against a wall or hang from the porch roof. Every day they dig up something or other. The place is an archaeological site. The creek that borders it is called Duck Creek. So Judy and Richard live at Duck's Bottom.

Rosey and I came bearing gifts – priceless copies of English newspapers, jars of Indian pickles, jars of Marmite. Richard wanted all the news from Britain, which meant who was reading the news for Channel 4, what was showing at the ICA, and what life was like since the 'Wicked Witch' had departed. We chewed the cud and chomped on the local staple of nachos and salsa sauce, and turned the box fan to Hi. The heat's embrace was beginning to turn a mite unfriendly. Judy informed us that the peach tree had just died and that groundhogs had been at the vegetable patch. And we were informed of Neville, a black snake who was in the habit of showing up in the shower or the kitchen cupboards. Finally we went to bed on the sleep-sofa our hosts had got from the Salvation

Army for $30. The bugs in it came at no extra charge. We kept the fan on but the sheets were sodden in seconds. Outside the orchestra of frogs and crickets rose to a crescendo and stayed there. Inside, mosquitoes, allowed access by rotting screen windows, feasted on our flesh.

In this neck of the rain forest the only true silence comes for about an hour after daybreak, when the night shift has finally called it a day and the cicadas have not yet cranked themselves up. But when they do, up there in the surrounding pines and tulip-poplars, the noise of a million scintillating, chirruping bugs soon becomes overwhelming. It's as though every telephone in the world is ringing for you. Circadian rhythm askew, I had woken early, in time to sample the quiet and the fresh, cool air, but when the aerial telephones started up I stuffed the soggy pillow over my head and retreated back to sleep. When I came to a couple of hours later the air was no longer cool but at least it smelt of coffee. Judy had fixed it, and it was weak. Back home for over a year now, she'd soon lost the European habit. Instead of downing one concentrated bombshell of caffeine to propel them through the day, Americans prefer a constant diluted drip-feed. I couldn't fault the bacon, eggs and grits, however. And after breakfast I went in search of my car.

Up the slope behind the shack, at the edge of the woods, was the little corrugated tin chicken shed where I had stored the Dodge three years before, unable to part completely with it, always intent on returning. And here I was at last. Disentombing the vehicle would be some work, however, because the crude doors to the shed had been thoroughly nailed up. As I tried to peel back a piece of tin, a number of red ants dropped off this and down my shirt and a yellowjacket buzzed threateningly around my head. I ducked and weaved and retreated down the slope in an effort to escape the wasp, and I shook the ants from my shirt and winced at their bites. Every movement I made was causing instant heavy-sweat breakouts, so humid was the day already. The earth was damp and sticky and clung to my boots as I stumbled about vainly warding off attacks from every ant and insect in the vicinity. I could have been wearing SkinSoSoft, of course – Judy's scented regular skin cream that she swore by as an insect repellent – but it was heavy and sticky and the smell repelled *me*. So I buttoned my shirt to the

wrists and neck, and, red-faced and dripping, I summoned
assistance. The others came with tools, and we hacked away in the
scorching, fetid heat like prisoners on the Burma Road. But finally
the tomb was opened. And there she was, as beautiful as ever, a
sleeping princess, in a thick patina of dust. Even her tyres were
still inflated. I gazed at her and remembered old times – driving
home drunk from a Greenville roadhouse ... Highway 61 in
Mississippi lined with telegraph poles like so many thousands of
crucifixes ... the rich scent of honeysuckle on the highways of
Alabama. Squeezing alongside and opening the driver's door, I
released the rich scent of must and mildew. It looked like the worn
patch on the driver's seat had rotted clean through. No matter, I
could soon fix that. I reached inside and tried the gear selector.
Well, it hadn't seized up yet, and neither had the steering wheel.
Things were looking good. I now had to check that the engine still
turned over. There was no battery so I'd have to rotate the fan. I
went round and lifted the hood and peered inside. There was that
wonderful, monstrous cast-iron motor again, and my heart leaped
at the sight. But then I saw that something was horribly wrong.
Every piece of wiring in that engine compartment – and there was
a great deal of it – had been ripped from its terminals, stripped of
insulation and mauled and mangled into a chaotic, useless mess. I
was staring at a very costly renovation job. I was also staring at the
lumps and wodges of straw which were spread liberally about the
engine. But – how? Why? Who? Or what? I consulted my hosts.

'Pack rats.' That was the answer I got. Pack Rats Ate My Car.
'They just love to chew wires and cables and things,' Judy
informed me. And they also love to make nests of straw. And if
they have any time left over from chewing wire and making nests,
why, they store up straw by stuffing it places. Packing it, rather.
First I saw hordes of rats, packs of them, but no. They're pack rats
''cause they pack stuff'. They sounded like neurotic rats to me. I
walked around the car and wondered what I could salvage from
my princess-murdered-in-her-sleep, and I winced from another
fact which had become clear: Judy thought these rats were *cute* – I
could tell by the way her green eyes lit up at the mention of the
fuckers. I opened the Dodge's trunk. The first thing I espied was
a number of wasp nests plastered around the sides like elegant
amphorae. Then I had the feeling I was being watched, and I

saw that I was. A large grey rat, a cartoon rat with a ludicrously long snout and big bobbly eyes plastered on as an afterthought, was staring at me. And I hate to anthropomorphize, but this rat was staring at me with indignation from her straw nest. I knew it was a her because she had a set of swollen teats and a couple of pink baby pack rats hanging upside down from them while engaged in some serious suckling. It was clear that Ma Packrat wanted me to git. Squatters' rights and all that. I closed the trunk and left her to it.

So the princess was dead and we would have to find a successor. Too sluggish from the trip and the climate-shock to spring into immediate action, we hung out for the rest of the day, reading, chatting, fending off insects. The clear, burning hot morning turned sultry around noon and segued into an afternoon of unremitting heavy rain drifting slowly over us from the mountains. This was to be the set pattern for the duration: monsoon heat and rolling thunder, a climate that doesn't encourage sustained periods of action of any kind. This is the nature of summer in these parts, and perhaps it has contributed to the general psyche of the South: a lot of thinking, followed by small bursts of activity, followed by another long bout of thinking. If you're not a thinking kind of person this can tangle your mind somewhat and lead to all sorts of crimes of passion and vengeance that the long hot summers of the South are famous for. True, there are air-conditioners and indoor jobs these days, but it doesn't stop the crime rate peaking in the hot season. Richard told us of a particular criminal who was currently on the loose here in Pickens County. An armed robber recently escaped from a chain gang. Name of Doyle Arthur Cannon. Now – there was a name which was obviously the result of some good old-fashioned southern thinking. I could see his Mom and Pappy sitting around on their porch for days – weeks – toying with that one, their eyes occasionally glinting, their thin lips curling, while the flies buzzed around their heads and a thousand telephones warbled in the tree-tops.

That evening we were invited to dinner by Judy's parents, Larry and Martha Keith. Their long, white timber bungalow stands on a steep slope above the road, shaded by redgum trees and surrounded by rhododendrons. At the top of the gravel drive stands

a white clapboard garage, above whose door hangs a basketball
hoop with the remains of a rotted old net. This feature alone offers
a clue to the nature of the residents here; because while every
regular American home sports a basketball hoop, it should be in
good condition, and, moreover, every regular American home
must also have in its front yard an American flag and, to complete
the insignia, a black mesh satellite dish. Basketball net, flag and
satellite dish. You see this triumvirate badge everywhere. Yes, sir,
the Holy Trinity: sport, nation, television. The Keith's effort would
not pass muster by these standards, in fact I wouldn't be surprised
if some folks actually took offence at that solitary tatty rag.

Larry is a slim, soft-spoken man in his late fifties. A
pronounced curvature of the spine makes him shorter than he
might be, and he has wide, feminine hips – upon which he is
inclined to rest his palms, thumbs pointing forwards, when he is
standing at ease. He has a boyish, freckled face, twinkling eyes,
thinning brown hair, and a bulbous nose whose pockmarks tell of
the ravages of alcohol. But Larry is dry these days, he has been for
a decade. Now he chainsmokes generic menthols and drinks vast
amounts of instant coffee. Back in his wild days, when his three
daughters were little girls, vodka was his poison, and he'd take
long solitary walks through the woods on his land, drinking as he
went. The tracks through the trees are still marked today by half-
buried, flat bottles of clear glass. Larry did a fair amount of
whoring, too. Judy tells of times when he'd ring home, drunk,
from some bed of easy virtue – she and her sisters would listen in
on the extension to their father's slurred tones and the giggles in
the background. And though they saw little of him in those days
they'd sometimes see him returning late at night, climbing out of
his Dodge Swinger and swaying up the garden path. He also had a
habit of reciting speeches from *King Lear* at the dinner table.
Those wayward days were certainly tough on the family, and clear
signs of repressed anger and resentment remain in the characters
of Judy and her two sisters. As to what crisis or combination of
circumstances might have sparked it all off, I can only speculate. It
may be that Larry felt intimidated by his elder brother, a whizz-kid
Nobel-prizewinning chemist, while he saw himself as a mere
country lawyer; it may have been the frustration of living in a
house full of females – he's been glad of Richard's company in

recent years and the pair of them often play chess late into the night. This visit, Larry's looking healthier, younger – he doesn't feel the need to attend Al Anon any longer; and he's finally got rid of his old Swinger.

Martha Keith is even quieter than her husband. Not a native Carolinian like Larry, she comes from a family of Connecticut Quakers, but a lifetime in the South has given her voice that down-home lilt. Days she works as a counsellor in a local social security office; evenings she makes tremendous meals, and this one was no exception. Larry served it up. He has a habit before he speaks of lightly clearing his throat, wobbling his head from side to side like a Hindu, and allowing himself a little smile:

'Uh, Judy, what is your *current attitude* t'ards asparagus?' he enquires meekly, aware of his daughter's pickiness and anorexic past. Judy had no problems with asparagus or anything else tonight. We tucked in to roast beef, corn meal finger bread, yellow squash, mushrooms, gravy, rolls, the said asparagus, fresh tomatoes with chives, ranch dressing, iced tea with fresh mint and lemon juice, blueberry crunch and vanilla ice-cream.

Afterwards we retired to the library and, passing through a small reception room en route, I was startled to see that television had finally made its debut here in the Keith household. I was disappointed. It meant that the last 0.00000001 per cent of Americans had now succumbed, and the national quota was complete. It was a modest little set, tucked discreetly in a corner. Larry says he got it to watch the football from time to time. He'll be repairing that basketball net soon at this rate.

Larry's library is a long, low-lit room furnished with nineteenth-century chairs and *chaises-longues*, a piano, a large maroon Persian carpet. Bookshelves line the walls from floor to ceiling, and speak of a classical education, a love of English literature, and an obsession with the life sciences. This night follows the typical after-dinner pattern here: it is basically an anything-and-everything seminar, with Larry as its leader. We sit around and smoke and drink coffee and say whatever comes into our heads when the spirit moves us (there can be some very long silences); and every so often the conversation will prompt Larry to rise and search his shelves, and produce some relevant or tangential information. Clearing his throat as if about to address

the court, he might give a brief introduction to the works of
Tacitus, or the memoirs of a Civil War officer, or a monograph on
some obscure beetle, before handing the volume respectfully to
whoever has stimulated its appearance, perhaps pointing out a
relevant paragraph with slightly quivering forefinger. That night I
had the dubious honour of receiving no fewer than three books
containing intimate details and illustrations of my car's assassin,
the Southern Rat, *Rattus australis*, or whatever it was called. I
imbibed the information through clenched teeth for what I judged
a polite period of time before rejoining the mainstream of the
conversation, which was now on the subject of testosterone, and
how Larry recently defended a company being sued by the Food
and Drugs Administration for selling the hormone as an
aphrodisiac. Judy had disappeared during this time, but she
returned shortly, interrupting an exchange between Larry and
Richard on the subject of James Joyce to present a jamjar
containing a baby toad, which she had slipped out to capture on
the driveway. The toad was duly examined by all and passed from
hand to hand, and the controversy concerning its exact species was
soon resolved by consulting the appropriate volumes on Amphibia
of the South-eastern United States.

Larry then treated us to the dossier on his current case – a set of
documents (morgue photographs, coroner's reports, police reports,
etc.) relating to a recent alleged murder in the nearby town of
Easley (or Sleazely as it is known locally – fifteen miles from
here). It concerned a feud between two related families of blacks:
an argument had flared up around midnight outside the Easley
McDonalds; a young man had got into his Chevy pick-up and
driven off, chased by his cousin who had jumped on to the running
board and was trying to get into the cab to continue the dispute.
The truck and the two men had sped up the road and turned into
the cemetery; and it was here that the pursuer had been thrown
from it and met his death. The police were claiming homicide:
they said that after his cousin had been thrown clear of the truck
the accused had deliberately driven the vehicle over him and killed
him. Larry held that death was due to the man cracking his head
on a tombstone as he fell from the Chevy. We were invited to
consider the evidence ourselves. There was the arresting officer's
report, the autopsy report with pictures and diagrams of the corpse,

description of stomach contents (which included 1.5 grams of cocaine), etc. And there were the statements of the witnesses: none had been present in the graveyard, but they all gave more or less the same story of an argument over a few dollars, and a man racing off in his truck with his cousin hanging from the door. The statements were all made by men and women in their twenties; they were all in immature handwriting, barely legible; and, strangely, each witness's brief biographical statement stated the degree of education they had achieved – 10th, 11th, 12th grade or college drop-out – as if they were applying for a job.

Crude though these statements were, I could hear the voices ringing out clear as a bell, and they were just as pathetic as the corpse in the Easley morgue. I once did a stint at a South London FE college, reading work on the same lined paper, in the same faltering handwriting, by black kids with the same tenuous futures as these witnesses to a stupid catastrophe. On this evidence at least, to try the kid for murder seemed a pointless exercise. Larry wasn't expecting any trouble securing an acquittal. Yet the cops were going ahead with it anyway. Hard not to conclude that this was because the kid was just another undereducated black with a record of petty crime; an expendable kind of character in America today.

I can't recall the process which led me shortly after this to be reading aloud a meditation by Andrew Marvell on gardens; or how we then got to talking about Church and State, and the rarity of a conquering army which will proselytize to its defeated opponents; and from there to the nature of hyenas – but by this time it was getting late, the others had drifted off elsewhere, and when Larry cleared his throat and said to me, 'Are you familiar with complex numbers?' I knew I had to bring the curtain down. Otherwise the patient, hour-long lecture he would surely have been glad to give would have taught me nothing and left me snoring. So the four of us said our goodnights and went down from the library of Academe to the trailer at Duck's Bottom.

Next day we got hold of the *Pickens Sentinel* and the *Greenville Times* and, after briefly noting in the *Sentinel* that Doyle Arthur Cannon was still at large, set about searching the classifieds for a successor to the murdered princess. You have to know the terminology. 'Loaded' means the car has a stereo which cost the seller a couple of hundred bucks and for which the price of the car has been upped by a couple of thousand. 'Runs Good' means it can't stop because the brakes are fucked. 'Good Gas Mileage' means petrol consumption is reasonable and you'll probably get as much as six miles to the gallon from your V12 50-litre Dinosaur, providing you can find regular leaded gas, which too has all but died out these days. 'Ford' means they're cheap to repair, but then again they always need repairing. 'Needs Some Attn' means a long, convoluted talk with the seller who will explain that this needs replacing, that needs regrinding, and the other is – you know anythin' bout cars? Well, it's this little thing that goes under the other thing that fits into the little hole underneath the first thing, and I haven't been able to find one because I just haven't had the time – but there's a wrecking lot on Highway 14 – or is it 25? – anyway, you won't have no trouble picking one up. What's that? Well ... no, actually, no – she won't run without it, yes that's correct ... and so on and so forth. And if you decide you're not interested, the man has always got another car he's selling on behalf of his sister: 'It's real clean ...' Everything but the exhaust, that is.

But America is bulging with old cars for sale, and there are plenty in the $500 range. And with every year that passes there are more and more decade-old Japanese cars on the market, and even the most patriotic citizen grudgingly admits their reliability, thus: 'Yep, you jest cain't kill 'em.' That's right. We nuked the devils back in '45 and look at them now, alive and kicking and running economic rings around us.

We did briefly consider the romantic attractions of a set of old Detroit wheels. But the few twenty-year-old indigenous models with a good reputation – the Dodge Darts, the Chevy Novas and the like – were now beginning to fetch collectors' prices. If they ran, which mine didn't. We decided to be realistic and bow to the new order. We spotted a Datsun 210 'in excellent running order' for $425 and the next day we borrowed the Toyota and went into Greenville to see it.

Greenville is the big city of upstate South Carolina. An undistinguished, messy kind of place surrounded by a cheap unregulated sprawl of tatty arterial roads and factories pumping out yellow fumes in the process of making whatever it is they make there. Like so many average-size cities of the South it has little identity: it looks defeated. It's easy to imagine that it has been this way ever since 'The War between the States', as they prefer to call that thing here. I once read the memoirs of a certain DeForest, a 'Union Officer of the Reconstruction', who describes the time he was quartered in Greenville. In 1867 a law of Congress sent soldiers to all the major centres of the beaten Confederacy to administer law and order until such time as the folks there could be trusted again. It was a belated attempt to stem the chaos and resentment that had broken out since the peace of two years earlier. Carpetbaggers and scalywags had descended from the north to buy up everything on the cheap and add insult to injury. People tended to hit out in frustration at anyone within reach, and especially the newly freed blacks, who weren't getting the freedom and justice due to them. DeForest found himself having to step in more than once to save a man unjustly accused of murder. He also had to deal with impoverished whites, and he describes an afternoon when he received a family of them, sharecroppers who had walked twenty miles across the county in bare feet and sackcloth to his office because they'd heard rumour of a handout. In Bible-righteous tones the soldier states how he listened politely to their pleas, told them they were mistaken, and sent them trudging home empty-handed. Eighty years later James Agee and Walker Evans visited the Deep South and documented those same kinds of people still living in one-room country shacks, still dressed in flour sacks, skull-faced and barefoot (*Let Us Now Praise Famous Men,* Houghton Mifflin, 1940). Nowadays of course things have changed; the South has partially 'risen again' as the bumper stickers proclaim it will – you only have to look at the glamour of Atlanta, CNN's company town – but you still don't have to look very far to catch the old mood: out in the sticks are the trailer homes, contemporary versions of the southern shack, sometimes solitary, sometimes clustered in little settlements – porchless, rectangular prefabs, tall TV aerials, gas bottle by the front step, pick-up truck on the dirt yard; rural *barrios* which will one day be valued by location scouts. And in town, the neglected streets; the decrepit housing (so many of the urban shacks are so tiny: the equivalent of a nineteenth-century Welsh miner's cottage); dead-eyed, mechanical humans; and everywhere sad little yard sales where people will sit all day in the hope of selling a busted TV, a few greasy cassettes and a couple of worn out car tyres. It's like the Third World. And after sundown as the resentment breaks out you hear the patrol cars' whoopee horns and you imagine all the liquor store hold-ups, the family feuds and domestic killings that you're going to read about in the next day's paper, as you tip milk on to the cornflakes and then see details on the carton of yet another missing young person – 'Have You Seen This Child?' – who like as not has been missing for years and may well by now be just a pile of dogmeat in some sad undiscovered serial killer's basement.

Driving to the edge of a downtown residential block, we found ourselves following a bumper sticker showing Saddam Hussein's face in a gunsight. Then we turned into the yard of a manufacturer of orthopaedic appliances. We saw a beige Datsun with its price whitewashed across the windscreen. Its vendor stood close by, and when we got out he came over to greet us. He wore shorts, and he walked awkwardly on an artificial leg. He introduced himself as Merton Sawyer III. He was a young, sad-faced man from Maine who had recently arrived in town to work at this here prosthetics factory.

'I hate selling cars,' he told us. I immediately had a good feeling about this deal. I gave the machine a hasty once-over, and then Rosey and I took turns to run it round the block. Apart from spongy brakes it seemed like a good one. A '79, with 125 thousand miles on the clock – a young engine by Japanese standards. It was the basic model – stick shift, no air-conditioning, no sign of a radio ever having been fitted, no fancifications whatever. The driver's seat was well-worn and tatty but the others looked as though they'd never had a bum on them in their lives. The car gave every sign of having been driven all its life by one or more quiet, solitary, careful, unimaginative dullards – an ideal history. The very colour alone was the biggest clue. My Dodge was the same anaemic tan, and that had come from an unassuming home-loving Idahoan vetinary scientist. Always buy from a bore. And the odd dent and spot of rust is good to find too, as was the case here – these trivia always lower the price handsomely.

Back at the lot we were about to commence the haggle when a pick-up truck swerved in at speed and drew up sharply. Its driver climbed down and greeted Merton Sawyer III jocularly. He was a tall middle-aged redneck in heavy boots, shorts, T-shirt and peaked cap. We were introduced to Merton Sawyer III's boss. 'London, England, eh?' he grinned at us. 'Yep, must pay it a visit one day,' he said, with zero commitment in his voice. Then he stared across the street to where a nun was walking up a driveway with her arms full of green globes. The man gave a chuckle. 'Lookit that,' he drawled. 'Them niggers sure love watermelons.'

Rosey said that she did, too.

'Well so do I,' he replied. 'But you know what I mean, heh, heh!'

I didn't know what he meant, but I had some ideas about what he was. And now he was leaving us. 'See ya later, Mert,' he called, as he strode into the building.

We told Merton Sawyer III that the car was fine except for the brakes and that we'd have to lay out much dough to get them up to scratch. This was his cue to hold out or come down. There was a silence while the Sawyer III brain ticked over. I was reminded of a haggle I had once witnessed by the side of a highway near Belgrade, en route to Greece by bus. One of our passengers, a tall German, had decided to buy himself a watermelon from one of the many watermelon-selling peasants strung out all along that road. The German asked the man his price but he couldn't understand the reply. Whereupon the peasant took out his knife and hacked out a figure on the skin of the watermelon. The German then shook his head vehemently and demanded the knife, with which he firmly obliterated the first figure before carving out a much lesser figure and handing back the knife. The peasant then scored out the German's figure and carved one slightly lower than his original. Thus it went: the knife was passed rapidly back and forth, pieces of melonskin and melonflesh flew everywhere, and eventually the two men's prices met in the middle. The German handed over his dinars and proudly took possession of the watermelon. He didn't seem to care that there was little left of it by now: it was devastated. It resembled the fields of Flanders by Armistice Day. It was mutilated, shapeless, skinless, soggy, and it was dripping all over his safari shirt as he took it to the bus in the manner of one who has won a famous victory. Yep, them Germans sure love watermelons.

Meanwhile Merton Sawyer III was still thinking. And Andy Soutter the First was wondering if the Datsun would end up covered in a mess of whitewashed figures. We waited, hoping he might come down by fifty dollars. But when he finally spoke he knocked it down by a hundred. So we immediately sealed the deal.

There is an excessive amount of bureaucracy involved in buying a car in America. For us, it began at a nearby bank where we had a bill of sale notarized, handed over the cash and received the car's title. We shook hands with the still melancholy vendor and parted company. Rosey drove off in the Datsun and I followed. We had our transportation. However, guarded joy turned to mild panic when Rosey reported wheel wobble at high speeds. So we wobbled tight-lipped into Pickens and had Larry's mechanic look it over. Luckily all that was needed was a set of used-but-good front tyres for fifty dollars. And the brakes were reckoned to have plenty of miles left on them for our purposes. So, wobble gone and rolling smoothly, we picked up the bureaucratic trail again. We rolled to the insurance office (Proud To Be American – The Gravely Agency) to get insured, thence to the courthouse to pay county tax, thence to the state Dept of Transportation to pay the state tax. Sixteen dollars, and the tag plate didn't even have a motto. North Carolina has 'First in Flight' commemorating the Wright Brothers; West Virginia has 'Almost Heaven' (except for coal mines and plagues of Gypsy Moth); New Jersey has 'The Garden State' (there's one somewhere); and they claim that 'You've Got A Friend In' Pennsylvania. But South Carolina is shy and keeps silent, although they have a picture of a small brown bird ('inaccurate' according to Judy). This was disappointing. If you've got a bit of history, why not flaunt it? I considered getting some Letraset and applying to our plate the motto 'First To Secede'. South Carolina was the first state to break away from the Union in 1860, thus precipitating the end of slavery for one thing – but since this came about more or less by accident, Lincoln himself admitting it was pure expedience, and since everything else the secession had precipitated hadn't been so beneficial, perhaps it wasn't such a good idea. Anyway, Americans aren't so hot on irony. We might unwittingly find ourselves leading a convoy of rise-again-and-hang-the-nigras men.

A day or so later we spent another afternoon in Greenville

when Richard and Judy took us on a tour of the thrift stores. They love getting things on the cheap. The only things they own which aren't second-hand are their toothbrushes. Thrift shops are usually twenty times bigger than British charity shops. They tend to use premises which were once supermarkets and are the size of aircraft hangars. This difference in scale can't just be put down to America's larger population. The used-goods market seems far too big for that, there's a disproportionate amount of stuff available. Well ... maybe there's more charity in America? Hard to measure, that. The other standard theory seems the best: people buy more new stuff and they get rid of it faster because they get bored with it sooner. If folks bought stereos to listen to or hats to keep the sun off or cars to get from A to B, it would be a different matter. But they don't. 'Utili-what?-ianism? That some kind of church?' So there are all these vast quantities of used cars, yard sales, second-hand shops, flea markets and thrift stores, all chock full of the multitudinous excrescences of good old consumer capitalism, going for a song. Good for the poor – the rapidly multiplying blacks, whites and hispanics – a Third World developing within the bosom of what still claims to be the most advanced of nations. Good also for another class of people with a set of entirely different values and aspirations who wander the same endless aisles of clothes-racks and household goods, people whom you could call the thrifty, or the ecologically responsible, or maybe just the slumming middle class – people like Richard and Judy, who do very well by these places, and even feed from them: the Salvation Army's Greenville store had a number of large hampers packed full of day-old bread, muffins and cakes – bushels of the stuff from which you could take two items for free with any purchase from the rest of the store. In this way I came out of there with a pair of nearly new cotton shorts and two large loaves of granary bread, having spent fifty cents. I felt silly. This discrepancy in value between the factory-fresh and the nearly new is enormous. What does it represent, this yawning gap, this value-void? Some great hole in the collective consciousness? A boredom index? A spiritual vacuum? An all-or-nothing mentality? Like the notices outside southern churches that proclaim 'Heaven or Hell – It's your Choice', no room for shades of grey where material things might find their true value. The gnostics have a notion about all matter being essentially evil – until it is imbued with spirit; looked at in this light, the item that is expensive when new and not long afterwards goes for a song seems equally forsaken at both stages of its life. It's said that the West puts too much value on material things, but it's equally true that they are undervalued as well. Cue: slides of non-renewable fossil fuels and ravaged rain forests along with my fifty-cent cotton shorts and day-old bread.

It was around this time that we realized we were supposed to be on holiday and that we might well do some holidaymaking. So the four of us walked in the woods, swam in the creek, and went fishing along the Saluda, hauling out rainbow trout and sunfish with worms and a bent pin in Huck Finn style; and we hung out at the trailer, Rosey and I still acclimatizing, reading *Day of the Locusts* and idly observing the snakes, the lizards, the skinks, the fence swifts, the humming birds, and the beautiful black-and-amber box turtles. And we met some more wildlife one night at a bar on Highway 11, a dark, quiet place populated by a handful of local *Rothälser*. Even though they're more reticent than most, southerners will always talk to you in a bar. The one that began talking to me wore the usual peaked cap, below which was a flat face of baby-smooth skin, a pair of beady eyes, and a thin, wide mouth set in a permanent smile. I wondered if I was looking at Doyle Arthur Cannon. He claimed to be from Kentucky, an ex-miner – but he looked too skinny to be a miner. He claimed to be a concreter now – but his hands were so smooth. And he told a joke whose punchline revealed that a deaf-and-dumb girl had been forcibly fist-fucked, heh-heh. Now I was certain he was Doyle Arthur Cannon, even though he called himself Tommy Slavin. The evening ended with 'Tommy Slavin', the proprietor and his wife in their tight marblewash jeans and teased hairstyles, and myself and Rosey, all hunched over the counter chewing on barbecued chicken wings and swapping jokes. I say swapping, but it was more or less one-way traffic. Rosey was silent, I managed one. Women and blacks didn't do too well out of these stories, but the young woman behind the bar redressed things somewhat for the last gag of the night, in which a boy and a girl brag and counter-brag about all the things they own. Finally the boy gets out his dick and declares that the girl can't match *that*. Whereupon the girl declares that she can always have as many of those as she wants. It raised a laugh; trouble is there is more than one way of looking at that kind of girl, and I was fairly certain about the way the men here were seeing her; although, in fairness, we didn't stay around any longer to find out.

The next day the *Pickens Sentinel* reported that Doyle Arthur Cannon had finally been apprehended. Not at a bar on Highway 11, but holed up – where else? – at his mother's shack, giving himself up without a fight. It seemed an appropriate moment to leave this corner of America, which was green and pleasant, but also mildly claustrophobic. Saying goodbye to Richard and Judy, I felt like Bilbo Baggins taking his leave of the Shire. In fact it is reported that old man Tolkien found many sources for his Hobbit books here in the South. The Carolinian writer Guy Davenport says that JRR got most of the names he used from local telephone directories; and it's true, this part of the world does abound with Brandywines, Tooks and Bagginses. And the misty mountains are never far away. Here at their south-western end the Appalachians are called the Great Smokies, and they rise up pretty suddenly from the gentle foothills of Pickens County only a few minutes north of Duck's Bottom. If you like mountains, these can be spectacular. At Pretty Place on the road to Brevard there is an extraordinary little chapel set on the edge of a steep north-facing precipice. It's built of timber and stone and has no north wall: you enter, look up the aisle and find yourself staring straight out over the cliff across a vast and deep wooded valley, and beyond this are layers and layers of ever-receding mountain ridges which turn from green to blue to all shades of terminal grey as they grow ever more distant. I WILL LIFT UP MINE EYES UNTO THE HILLS is the motto carved into a roof beam which captions the spectacle. I found the large wooden cross erected on the parapet somewhat diminished my sense of awe – it seemed an inappropriate place for a torture instrument; but the place was a chapel after all, and one could always step up between the cross and the cliff edge to get the secular view, always riskier really.

To follow the Appalachians up to the cities of the north-east you can either take the Blue Ridge Parkway, a modest-sized tourist trail laden with viewing points, picnic spots and information centres; or you can take I-81 which is equally spectacular,

especially where it passes through the Shenendoahs in Virginia.
We opted for neither. We decided to take the shortest route to the
coast and then head up the eastern seaboard. Wishing us *bon
voyage*, Larry warned us against taking too many freeways.
Standing on his driveway, wearing a baseball cap and holding a
dibber, he smiled, lowered his eyes, and wobbled his head: 'The
interstates are – ahem – uh, *singularly unenlightening*,' he said.

2. I was Ceaucescu's Chauffeur

For the meantime we eschewed Larry Keith's advice and, after filling up at the Greenville Hess station, we took I-85, which led us rapidly into North Carolina and past the cities of Charlotte, Kannapolis, Greensboro and Durham. By nightfall we were thirty miles or so from the Virginia line, and we turned off the interstate and drove a few miles further into the small town of Oxford. It was a one-motel town, but fortunately this motel was the kind we were looking for: a small semicircular terrace set around a gravelled and potholed forecourt where a couple of beat-up gas-eaters were parked; at one end of the building a Pepsi machine stood like a sentinel, glowing out of the darkness. At the other was the office, displaying a neon VACANCY sign in its window. We went in. We found ourselves in a small cubicle like a miniature bank, facing a counter which was screened off by tinted, and very possibly bullet-proofed, glass. The cubicle smelt of patchouli.

'Yes?' said a voice from behind it. The face was invisible. We enquired after the price of a room for two. 'Twenty-three dollars plus tax,' said the Anglo-Indian voice, and then a brown hand slid the form to us under the glass. Rosey asked the man if he was from England. No, but he had family in Bradford.

There are hundreds of these older-style motels, especially those in the South, which are now run by Indian and Pakistani immigrants. In Britain the ailing businesses they have taken over are the cornershops; in the States they are the small, run-down motels whose business has declined since the interstates bypassed their highways. They have lost trade to the newer, multistorey chains which sprang up hard by the new freeways – the Days Inns, the Budget Hosts, the Best Westerns and the like. But the Asians have come and bought them for a song and made going concerns of them – you very rarely see these places lying derelict. They don't always have the amenities of their modern counterparts – the rooms may not have telephones or forty channels of cable TV, and if there's a pool, chances are it will be filled with dirt and functioning now as a potato patch – but they're cheaper, usually just as clean, and more often quieter. Sometimes, however, you will come across one of these old-time 'auto courts' or 'motor inns' with its period sign likely as not consisting of an extravagant neon arrow encircling the name and pointing to the terrace of rooms or the clutch of detached miniature bungalows, but which also has a more recent notice attached which reads 'American Owned'. What this actually means is 'White Owned'. It also means you're going to have to pay more for the dubious privilege of staying there and being able to salute Old Glory in the morning, which you will find hanging above the office door.

Meanwhile, here at the Crown Motel in Oxford, we filled in the form, handed it back with our money, and the besieged hand passed us the room key. We decamped into our room – brown carpet, brown bedspread, brown wallpaper and faded brown print on the wall depicting an (American) Indian hunting buffalo – switched on the air-conditioner to dispel the monsoon-like climate, and went out again to find a place to eat.

Oxford was a tired, dusty old crossroads township that had seen better days – or at least busier ones before I-85 killed most of its *raison d'être*. We had but two choices: we could eat in the Pizza Hut by the window, or we could eat in the Pizza Hut along the back wall. Extravagantly, we took the window seat and watched a large Mexican family celebrate one of their kids' birthdays with party hats and deep-dishes all round. Three years ago you didn't see Mexicans in this part of the world; but since the recent amnesty they have a higher profile all over the States. They are even taking over the Mexican restaurants.

After our first refreshingly air-conditioned and bug-free night in America we were away early in the morning, and were soon at the state line. WELCOME TO VIRGINIA, the sign said, SO MUCH TO LOVE. This sentiment alone told us we were still in Dixieland (you couldn't really imagine it heralding a drive into New Jersey, or Utah), but Virginia is a different flavour. The countryside is more cute: no desolate swathes of heathland sprouting chimneystack

ruins of shotgun shacks; the grass is a deeper green, the
weatherboard is a glowing white. You could say we had passed
from the Deep South to the Shallow South. It is further north in
this state that things start to appear a mite less Anglo and a little
more Saxon – in the Dutch (i.e. Deutsch) Country, which
advertises itself with icons of olde-worlde pastoralism (commonly
a farmer's wife in bonnet and clogs holding a basket of apples
redder than poisoned ones in fairy tales) and expands into
Pennsylvania, where there is a preponderance of old-European-
style puritan communities (as opposed to the born-again-in-
nylon style of Deep Southerners): in-bred groups with names like
Stoltzfus, Wenger and Kling whose favourite colour is black and
who believe that since their Bible says nothing about the
Enlightenment, the Industrial Revolution or the All-new-for-'92
Toyota Pick-up, why then they'll have nothing to do with these
things neither; self-sufficient clans of Mennonites, tens of
thousands of them, dedicated to the idea of Toil, all dressed up
from the wardrobe of *Mother Courage* and equally fitted to pose
for Grant Wood's *American Gothic*. There is a severity which
leaks out beyond the bounds of these antique folk, a certain
exemplary force, one which I had encountered three years earlier
en route from Duck's Bottom to New York City with Ffarington
and the Dodge (then known as Mabel, in honour of her impending
entry into New York society).

At that time we were on the scenic route, I-81, which comes up
from Tennessee: up mountain, down mountain and all along the
rolling ridges, listening to *All Things Considered* (National Public
Radio's superior version of the BBC's *PM*) and trying to keep
coked-up *Rothals* truckers off our tail; driving in packs, well over
the puny speed limit, hoping that one of us had a fuzz-buster and
wasn't afraid to use it despite repeated roadside warnings that
radar detectors were anathema in this state of the union. (The
Virginia cops had fuzz-buster-busters. No doubt some son of
Hazzard was already perfecting a fuzz-buster-buster-buster; that's
progress.) Somewhere north of Roanoke, the blue ridges to our
right, the Shenendoah Valley falling away westwards, we pulled
into a rest center and witnessed an earnest theological debate
taking place in the washroom lobby between a tall Judaic type
(beard, skullcap, shorts, penny loafers) and a group of waspy

Christians. For reasons best known to themselves, they were taking apart the book of Baruch. But it made a change from Revelation, which was the standard material further south for such discussions: in restaurants, on buses, on street corners, one was always coming across these impromptu seminars at which the prospect of fire, plague and the Lord's vengeance would be gleefully entertained.

Another hour up the road, another hour closer to Death & Judgement, we turned off the interstate and made our way along lesser highways which wound through the forested foothills: holiday motels with clock golf and go-kart tracks sitting in clearings; restaurants offering 'Dutch Cooking'; farm produce for sale by the highway; gravelled switchback roads and a blue evening mist rising from the tree-tops. At the point where four states converge around this placid corner of the Alleghenies, we crossed into West Virginia and began to take roads of rapidly declining status until we were kicking along a narrow dirt track, steep and winding and densely wooded, which led us presently to a modern, two-storey timber house in a small clearing, hemmed in by tall, straight-trunked trees backlit by the diffuse glow of a mellow pink sunset. This was the home of an old theatrical buddy of Ffarington's, 'T.P.' Huhn.

Upon arrival at a host's house in America, amidst all the greetings and journey-talk, part of my mind is always checking out the situation as regards vice. In other words, to what extent and with what varieties do these people indulge, if at all, and to what extent and with which varieties would one be permitted to indulge oneself? Part of the postmodern condition seems to be a pluralistic multiplicity of social conventions, with constant variations and updates of standards and attitudes. And I never put much faith in that old 'Mi casa – su casa' business. If these people knew anything about my house they might not make such a rash equation. These vices do include such things as leaving your shoes on indoors or pissing in the sink, but it's mainly a question of Substances. Richard and I had arrived with a fair old complement – alcohol, tobacco, Do-Do's (ephedrine) from Boots in Camden Town, caffeine in our bloodstream, and five gallons of evil leaded gas in the Dodge's tank. We were wide open to censure. Ffarington didn't have much briefing intelligence since he hadn't seen his friend for ten years; all I knew was that Huhn, his spouse and child called themselves vaudevillians and were always on the road touring shows they wrote, playing schools and community centres.

Well, here's a *mezuzah* at the door – good sign or not? And here are the Huhns – and they've got their shoes on. There's T.P., chubby, cropped hair, a friendly blond bear; there's Sarah, taller, dark, dungaree'd, weatherworn face, heavy-jawed countenance; and there's the kid, a skinny, pale, platinum-blonde girl who's seven years old and whose name is Happy. (Happy, we later learned, did the family's accounts and tax returns.) A meal was waiting for us in the wood-stoved-and-natural-pine kitchen, which was in one corner of this open plan, barn-like building whose upper storey was a boxed-in gallery, with most of the ground floor being a rehearsal studio. We offered the wine we'd brought along. Sarah said they didn't really drink, but T.P. persuaded her to allow the indulgence, and we all got merry over meat pie and salad. My 'Beautiful part of the country here' was Sarah's cue to tell us about all the shit that the nearby mining industries were putting in the earth and the air, and about the plague of gypsy moths busy killing their trees, and of the fearsome prospect of the denizens of killer bees which were slowly working their way over from the south-west. 'Yep,' chimed in T.P., 'almost Heaven.'

As I'd surmised, tobacco was *non grata*, so after the meal I excused myself and stepped outside for a smoke. A minute later Ffarington joined me, fumbling over the Marlboros; and a short while after this T.P. joined us under the stars and ushered us conspiratorially round the back, where he rolled a small reefer by torchlight. He'd gone along with Sarah and cut out tobacco and most of the drink from his life, but he retained this activity in secret. Presently we were three euphoric shadows, joking and reminiscing in the chilly dark.

The immediate neighbourhood, as I discovered the next morning, bore an even closer resemblance to Tolkien's Shire than did Duck's Bottom: miniature gravel roads rambling past water meadows; a little wooden bridge over the creek where a knot of water snakes basked on a rock; a scattering of clapboard houses and small farmsteads. JRR would not have mentioned Sarah and Happy skinny dipping in the lake, however: in his world the female kind is conspicuously absent. At the edge of this tranquil mere, idyllic with greenery and morning sunshine, the Huhns saw fit to be severe with a stranger, a young man basking in his Y-fronts on the little wooden jetty. Firmly but just-about-politely they enquired as to what he was doing here on private land, politely listened to his flimsy friend-of-a-friend-of-a-friend connection, politely insisted that he leave, and politely watched him get dressed and depart. The community had been defended. A short while later Ffarington and I took our leave in a mutual photo-session back at the house. My picture of the Huhns shows the three of them standing with their backs to the breezeblock and timber of their self-built home. It's an updated version of *American Gothic*: admittedly the house lacks pointed-arch windows and neither adult holds a pitchfork, but we have a tall dark one in dungarees next to a shorter, blond one: they could be grandchildren of the folk in the painting with the expression that says 'I worked for this land and built this house with the sweat of my brow and the help of the Lord and things happen around here on *my* terms.' T.P. and Sarah are smiling into the sun, arm-in-arm in the modest, rough-lawned yard of their sparely furnished home; there is something tempered about their joy: traces of struggle, engagements with demons. Sarah's face, like the farmer in Wood's icon, is tough and determined, and it is she who wears the overalls; while T.P.'s expression, like the farmer's wife, is just a mite shadowed by some anxiety. I wonder what that farmer's wife did for her secret vice.

This time around Rosey and I left the interstate early on and headed east towards the coast on Highway 58, a gentle switchback through grassy, wooded countryside passing through quiet old towns like Brodnax and Radium. These strange names abound in America; having already been to Social Circle, Georgia and Defeated, Tennessee, I didn't think I could be surprised anymore, but there is always something weirder up ahead.

A hundred miles of 58 brought us to Norfolk, where Chesapeake Bay opens out to the Atlantic. From here we crossed to Virginia's Eastern Shore via the Chesapeake Bay Bridge Tunnel, an eighteen-mile stretch of road that alternately spans the bay and then dives beneath it a number of times for the benefit of shipping; it's an exhilarating ride. In the middle section of the bridge is a tourist centre where we stopped awhile to admire the view – basically a lot of grey water in every direction – while the conning-tower of a large submarine swept by us. Inside the tourist shop Rosey forced me to pose and pull various brain-damaged faces whilst wearing a souvenir peaked cap – one of those things worn by 90 per cent of American males which have a mesh top, a little adjustable backstrap, and a front end rearing squarely up like a giant billboard; indeed, most of them are produced solely for the benefit of advertising anything from baseball teams to farm machinery distributors to slogans like 'A Country Boy Can Survive' embossed across a confederate flag. Rosey has christened them 'meat hats'. Gung-ho, all-American. They look German to me, however; just add a little chinstrap, and what have you got? – a brownshirt helmet. I don't enjoy these objects, and was glad to replace this one on the shelf once my spouse had taken her snaps.

Highway 13 is straight and flat and runs up the narrow spit of land that is the Eastern Shore; it runs thus for sixty miles or so, and every five miles is a farm shop selling VIRGINIA HAMS. Pork country, and plenty of pigs to be seen too. Other stores were selling WATERMELONS PEANUTS GIFTS GUNS. And just a few miles north of Temperanceville, Dixieland ends at the Maryland line, and it ends quite visibly: suddenly there are giant liquor stores everywhere: brightly lit, gaudy emporia which, unlike their southern counterparts, are not trying to make one feel ashamed at wanting to purchase spirits. In the South, these places are often small, unobtrusive little establishments, dimly lit little 'package' stores where the atmosphere is laden with guilt and you carry out your brown paper parcel like some item of heinous pornography. Ordinary bars, like the one we visited on Highway 11, don't have a spirit licence; it's strictly beer, but this doesn't prevent them being widely stigmatized. For example, when I had been introduced by Ffarington to one of the Keith's tenants, farmer's wife Hettie Finch (blue-rinse, Buick, bungalow, and lurid livingroom with monster TV in baroque-palatial mahogany cabinet), this cheerful woman gave us news of her daughter's recent engagement. The son-in-law elect was a soldier at the camp in Biloxi, Mississippi, and the pair had met in a bar down there. 'Mind you,' said Hettie Finch, shifting in her florid armchair and feigning an expression of puzzled innocence, as if the thought had just then occurred to her, 'I sure don't know *what* she was doing in a *bar*.' Of course she didn't.

You don't see pornography openly for sale in the South, either; but here in urban Maryland, every other store was proclaiming sex or alcohol; and, unsurprisingly, many of the cars parked outside them carried Virginia plates. At Pokomoke City we celebrated by buying a large bottle of rum, which we parked in the trunk of the car. Rules vary from state to state, but you're usually breaking one or more laws if you carry alcohol in the passenger compartment, whether the can or bottle is open or not. I'm not sure whether pornography comes under similar statutes, but the same thing doesn't apply to your loaded firearms, of course – man's got a right to defend himself against ... well, drunken sex fiends, I guess.

Around 10 o'clock that evening we drove into Salisbury (pop. 15,302) and scouted around for accommodation. During this search we pulled off the busy highway for a few seconds to change drivers. We swopped seats in a house driveway and immediately drove off back towards the downtown from where we'd come. Less than a minute later there were all sorts of coloured lights flashing crazily in the rearview mirror, so I pulled in to the side of the road and we both got out to see what the police wanted with us.

The cop was short and fat, and his shoulder badge proclaimed FRUITLAND. He told us that the old lady in whose driveway we had stopped had been robbed six times in the last few weeks and had called 911 as soon as she'd heard our tyres on her gravel. But he was instantly placated by our credentials – i.e. our British voices – and apologized for the inconvenience. I then made the mistake of asking him if he knew anywhere good to eat down the road in Salisbury. He took a lot of time and trouble over a simple set of directions. 'Got that?' he said finally. 'Yes, lovely, thanks,' we said. 'Well, I'll just go over it again to make sure,' he said, and he did. And we thanked him, said goodnight and turned towards our car. But: 'I was in England once,' he piped up, 'I have a good friend there. He's a retired admiral of the Navy. Lives at Port's Mouth. Do you know Port's Mouth?'

'Afraid not.'

'Oh well ... anyway, let me just give you those directions again

...' and he did, while we stood there tired and hungry. I wondered if one gave out extra charisma in states of fatigue and famishment and whether it was this that was making a sycophant of this policeman. My lungs were filling with the exhaust fumes from his vehicle; my eyes were sore and dazzled by its lights and those of the traffic rushing noisily past us a few feet away. The Fruitland cop burbled on exuberantly. Was he angling for a tip, or what? Twenty minutes had passed by without news of a single crime crackling in on his radio, pray for one though I might – and that must be some kind of record. But eventually our ordeal at the hands of the fruitcake cop was over, and we drove away back into downtown Salisbury.

Outside a three-storey building called the Thrift Motel, a bored hooker sat on a wall. In the parking lot, a man was asleep at the wheel of a regular pimp's chariot: a seventies' Cadillac with a front end like a chrome-plated version of Chartres Cathedral: we squeezed into the small space between this and the door of the room we were checking in to, and, having dumped our bags and taken a swift shot of rum, left again to find the eating place so well described to us that entering it was like greeting an old friend: it was cheerful enough, a cosy little bar-cum-restaurant with a friendly young bar-tender who told us that he was an actor, and that we had been unlucky to have just missed the local Shakespeare Festival, which had been 'a blast'. At one end of the bar the regulation TV showed the regulation baseball game, and as we snacked I watched the game and wondered: what was so German about baseball? It wasn't just those caps they wore. I couldn't put my finger on it.

Flicking through the TV channels later on back in our motel room, I reflected on the current state of the union. Compared to three years ago, when Reagan was still on the throne and her husband was still President – or 'Presnightstates' as the post is called here – and the recession had not come home to roost, America now had a more desperate air about it, something that the recent victory in the Gulf War had not been able to dispel. Unemployment and the national debt were both rising alarmingly; comparative tests were putting American students bottom of international league tables; and the health care crisis was beginning to get big coverage: ordinary working people, as opposed to the rich or those on welfare benefits, were running scared of the medical profession – most of them didn't have insurance, and one major operation or a series of treatments was leaving people in hock to the hospital for the rest of their lives. The big banks were going bust: there was the Savings & Loan scandal, and the BCCI affair which showed who was really making the money out of the illegal narcotics trade. As for the 'war on drugs', that was a pathetic non-starter: drug-related crime was booming. 'Just Say No'? You couldn't devise a more feeble slogan if you tried. And here now was Milwaukee's mass killer Jeffrey Dahmer stalking into the courtroom in his red jump suit. It was as though Ronald McDonald had taken off his make-up to reveal the hideous truth below the saccharescent surface of things.

Alright, so that was the news – I flipped across to a comedy show, stand-up comedians doing their stuff; what was their angle on all this? What incisive satire would I find here, cutting through all the crap? Well, er, there are a lot of jokes about fucking; and a lot of gags about how crappy this TV show is, or that Hollywood movie was; and more about this TV personality, or that movie star. And you won't get most of them if you don't regularly watch that crappy show or this silly star. No, the comics were as smug about it all as the televangelists, who were as busy as ever on their own channels. And *their* current complaint is that there's not enough religious material on prime time TV. And what spiritual guidance do they have to offer? They're still out to prove that Armageddon is all set for the Middle East a very short time from now, and if you don't know about it, you haven't got a chance, so send twenty dollars for their explanatory video right away.

Hell, though – gas was still cheap, wasn't it? So we must be doing something right. In the morning we filled up across the road and headed for New York.

Around lunch time, halfway through Delaware, we stopped for a break. Unable to find an ordinary diner we went into a McDonalds. I wasn't understood when I asked for water – I'd forgotten that you have to say 'wuhter'. Sitting here, we observed a couple of women a few tables away dressed like sixteenth-century German peasants, chomping burgers and sucking on milkshakes. There was a fat one and a thin one. They wore simple white cloth caps, and long navy-blue cotton dresses buttoned – or rather pinned – up to the neck, and had stout old-fashioned shoes. And the thin one was clearly pregnant. Were these Amish folk, we wondered? Could be. On the other hand, there wasn't much that was archaic about a Big Mac and fries. But if they were Amish, we reasoned, they'd have a horse-drawn buggy waiting outside – wouldn't they? When they had finished their meal, we followed them out. In the parking lot we watched disappointedly as the two women climbed into a bright orange Chevrolet panel van and drove away.

These, then, were heretical Mennonites, sometimes known as 'black-bumper' Amish, or, in this case, 'burger-and-fries' Amish, too. Clearly, as a result of assiduous Bible study, they had discovered a reference to automotive transport and had therefore sanctioned its use. Perhaps the fiery chariot in which Elijah ascended to Heaven was in fact an orange Chevy van? Perhaps Christ rode into Jerusalem not on a donkey but in a Mustang convertible? And perhaps Moses crossed the Red Sea – merely a stretch of marshland in the dry season – in a convoy of hi-sprung four-wheel-drives?

Mennonism is quaintly attractive as a museum piece. But total archaism can also be seen as a paranoid state and a dangerous model. We should be colonizing space by now, have found a cure for cancer, etc. etc., yet here are a 'worthy' people still obsessed with sixteenth-century technology and determined to kill joy at its source. The black-bumper Amish may have compromised on automobiles, but with what relish do they blot out worldly delights when painting over every square inch of decorative chrome on their vehicles, and, for their garments, eschewing the vanity of buttons in favour of hook fasteners! The Amish are attractive because their communities appear to be models of social control: stable, peaceful, self-sufficient; but at what cost? Innovation, pleasure, sexual and gender freedoms go up in smoke for the sake of some patriarchal pipedream. We were just fifty miles or so from the Amish heartland over in Lancaster County, Pa., from highways reportedly clogged with tourist traffic and (non-Amish) gift shops. Travel writers and other commentators, after visiting this area, insist that these folk should be 'left in peace', but the Mennonites' extraordinarily crude and high-profile attempt to arrest the flow of time in deference to some idea of the eternal and the carved-in-stone is bound to attract attention. Since they act like royalty – defenders of the faith, special costumes and nineteenth-century carriages – they should expect such attentions. But we left them alone just the same.

By mid-afternoon we'd crossed the Delaware River and were speeding along the New Jersey Turnpike in the blazing heat. New Jersey does have gardens, of course – it's only when you get close to New York that the landscape turns mucky and sulphurous – but again, you don't get to see much of the green and pleasant business because the freeway is thickly lined with tall evergreens. After two hours, however, you get a startling full-frontal view of Manhattan for the final ten miles of elevated section. As the turnpike descended towards the Hudson and the Datsun bumped and lurched over the cracks and potholes of the wrecked roadway, its concrete rotten and brown as nicotine, the great city rose up before us like a giant financial bar graph. We slipped through the Lincoln Tunnel's grubby, ceramic embrace and prepared to run the gauntlet of stop-light panhandlers and vehicular assault teams armed to the teeth with foaming sponges.

We were staying in an apartment on the upper east side. We unpacked the car of absolutely everything, because no vehicle is safe in this city. Cars display specially printed signs on their windows: THERE IS NO STEREO IN THIS CAR; and on the trunk: THERE IS NOTHING IN MY TRUNK; just the latest variations of those please-don't-rob-me notices already commonplace outside liquor stores and gas stations warning of the penalties for such behaviour or declaring that the safe is time-locked; although it seems hard to credit such signs on the windows of large banks which announce that there is NO CASH KEPT ON PREMISES – and I've seen these, I swear. So we took out the radio, which was easy since it was just duck-taped to the floor, and we left nothing in the trunk but two styrofoam coolers and a quart of oil.

Our host was a young Englishman who had been at school with Rosey's sister and was now a whizz-kid in the publishing world. But his fancy title, he was quick to point out, didn't mean he earned that much, and he offered the size of his apartment – one small room, kitchen and bathroom – as visible proof. Sure, it was a security block in a middle-class neighbourhood, but if he'd so much as put a bookcase in the living room you would have had to move around sideways in there, as was already necessary in the bathroom, kitchen, and two-foot hallway, which is where Tom *had* stashed his hundreds of books. The sole large item of furniture was a sleep-sofa; which would only have to put up the two of us since Tom would be staying the next three nights with 'my friend Joolie,' as he put it, his accent already this side of the mid-Atlantic and closing in fast. Tom's ambition, like so many Manhattanites, was to eventually save enough to buy himself somewhere in the country upstate and commute to work, maybe only a couple of days a week, doing the rest of his business from home-based screens and machines. Which was why he wasn't renting a more fancy apartment right now. So Tom showed us where everything was (for which purpose he didn't have to move from his spot), arranged to meet us the next day for a meal, and left us to it.

Tom's kitchen was a treat: a pre-war job, with the fridge, sink and all the fittings displaying those characteristic curved edges; it was the sort of kitchen that Tom the cat first chased Jerry mouse around in, in those early cartoons with their lovingly watercoloured-washed backgrounds, when Tom's face was nastier, fatter, and had two vicious side teeth always protruding from his mouth. Wilder days; and since then, like the cartoons, kitchens have become sanitized and harder-edged. But plenty of the old ones still survive, as do all sorts of different kinds of equipment, from Zippo lighters to Bakelite ashtrays to gothic-looking air-conditioners to period diners, motels and automobiles. This is the 'If it ain't broke don't fix it' ethos which sits paradoxically alongside all that famous planned obsolescence. It's particularly noticeable in America's store signs and shopfronts and company logotypes: compared to the British in particular, Americans seem so much more secure with their public image; they don't have the neurotic compulsion to carry out a corporate redesign every couple of years. It's a peculiar thing about America that for a country where the future so often reveals itself first, so much of the past is still visible. Like the German coffee shop a couple of blocks away where we ate that evening, in which everything – even the menu with its comfort-food of boiled potatoes and chicken in thick gravy with mushy peas – appeared to have been preserved unchanged for at least sixty years.

You find none of this archaism in Britain, apart from a few cathedrals and castles, and a number of Edwardian pubs which have been done up to look Victorian. It's as though each successive political regime has been dedicated to wiping out all traces of life as lived under its preceding opponent: for example, no set of mundane commercial premises now gives any hint that it might have existed before 1979. America's political swings are usually less drastic, and betray no such fundamental desires to break with the past. Or it could simply be that having less of a past at their disposal, they are husbanding it more carefully than other nations might. This doesn't always work out so quaintly when it comes to certain attitudes such as the one regarding firearms, which leaves Americans dying every hour of every day; and the one regarding industrial practices, which is leaving American enterprise dead in the water; but for tourists of the mundane, innocent trappings of life, it's fine. Apart from all those *I Love Lucy* reruns, that is.

The next day, while Manhattan went about its business in ninety-degree heat, we slept in, and in the afternoon we decided to take advantage of the residents' laundry to wash a fortnight's worth of sweat and grime out of our clothes. We took the lift down to the basement. Its doors opened upon a dark passage lined with grey breezeblocks. Nearly opposite us was a small laundry room. We piled our clothes into the washing machine, and slotted in a few quarters to set it rumbling. Then we turned to go back to the apartment while it did its stuff; but we found the doorway blocked by a distinctly unfriendly-looking mongrel dog, who stared at us for a second or two before beginning to bark loudly and slowly advance upon us. It was a black, mangey beast; its ribs were showing, its eyes were bloodshot, and its tail showed no sign of wagging, no matter how many chummy hello-there's I offered it. Rosey had already climbed on to a dryer for refuge, and I was about to do the same, when the animal's owner appeared in the doorway: a short, fat man in shorts and a filthy black T-shirt, with an unshaven, rough-hewn face whose complexion was in worse condition that the concrete on the New Jersey Turnpike. His wild eyes darted back and forth between the pair of us as he stood there in the doorway, trembling.

'Will you call your dog off, please?' I asked politely.

'What are you doing here? Who are you?' he shouted back in a
gutteral mid-European voice.

'Please call the dog off,' I entreated. The hound was now sizing
up my calves and deciding which one it would feast on first.

'Who are you? What are you doing here?' replied the man,
taking a half step backwards at the sound of my voice. He was
now beginning to shake more violently than we were.

'We're friends of Tom's – Tom Lichfield – second floor ...
we're doing our laundry,' I said, thinking that perhaps a statement
of the obvious might have some effect. It didn't. I retreated on to
the top of the second dryer. The dog barked some more.

'I know everyone here – I am superintendent,' he said, raising
his quivering voice above the noise of the dog. 'Who are you?
What are you doing here?'

This fruitless pattern of exchange went on for some while
before the creature finally saw fit to call off the other creature. I
dropped back to the floor from my perch. Immediately the
concrete-faced janitor took a step backwards and held out his arm
in a defensive gesture: 'You wait – you wait!' he blabbed. We
then explained once more, from our perches, who we were and
what we were doing here. The man craned his neck in the
direction of the throbbing washing machine. 'What are you doing
with my machine?' he demanded tremulously. Once more I
explained that we were friends of Tom Lichfield. 'Look,' I said,
fumbling in my pocket, 'we've got Tom's key. Apartment 2D.'
And I produced the brass latchkey and held it up.

The wild-eyed janitor reacted as though I had pulled a 45
Magnum on him. He lurched backwards and once more threw out
his hands with spread palms, peering at me through the fingers.
After a moment or two he seemed to have convinced himself that
the key was not a weapon of violence. Hesitantly, he stepped
towards me, and then in a sudden move, reached out and grabbed
the key before retreating just as quickly. Then he fondled the
thing, and his eyes grew soft and sentimental:

'I know all the keys here. I have all the keys,' he said. 'I check.'

And he did. He pulled out a bunch of keys from his pocket, and
eventually ascertained that we did indeed possess keys to an
apartment in his building. And he eventually also seemed to recall
the name of our host from the recesses of what seemed to be a

memory dimmed substantially by constant daily doses of alcohol. And, bit by bit, this paranoid, bloodshot-eyed subterranean lost enough of his terror of unknown faces lurking his domain to eventually enable him to converse with us in a manner that came perilously close to the normal. The ghastly hound now lurked some way back in the shadows of that breezeblocked passage; we climbed down from our perches – but carefully and slowly, for the least sudden movement on our behalf still produced terrified keep-away-from-me-I've-got-a-starved-wild-animal-here-and-I'm-not-afraid-to-use-it gestures from our trembling host. We knew we had to be very polite in this situation. He had the dog and he had the key to our apartment, after all. And he was clearly suffering from irrational fears, and therefore unpredictable and dangerous. For all we knew, he might have had some firearm within reach, or some crazed companion lurking in the shadows of these dim catacombs. But there was no doubt that by now he was considerably calmer, and he began to tell us of all the responsibilities of his job – the garbage-clearing, the used-newspaper collecting, the blocked-drain-clearing, and so forth, in an effort to boost his standing in the sight of we two strangely accented interlopers.

But what makes a man so afraid? There's many an alcoholic, and many a building superintendent considerably more self-possessed than this jumpy fellow. And New York City is not such a lurid hellhole as to turn every one of its inhabitants into quivering messes of grey-fleshed gollums. The answer became clear as he spoke. He was Romanian. And his story might have been titled: *I Was Nicolai Ceaucescu's Chauffeur*. For such he claimed to have been.

What had brought him to this illustrious post we were never to find out, so garbled was the man's tale. But if you spend five years driving a paranoid murdering lunatic around, some of it's clearly going to rub off. One can scarcely imagine a more touching scenario, except perhaps one entitled *I Was Margaret Thatcher's Relief Masseur*. Imagine sitting at the wheel of a long black Zil limousine, within inches of that deluded maniac, Ceaucescu, that is, engulfed in his aura for hour after hour, within close earshot of a million pathetic fears; taking a different, tortuous and twisted route to work every day for fear of ambush or betrayal; driving to and fro from government buildings to pretentious palaces, and

thence to the village of your forebears to make sure the place had
been completely evacuated and destroyed; what conversations he
must have heard; what twisted logic; what violent, fearful,
statements: Stop here, the road may be mined; Go this way –
that'll surprise them; If I'm not back within two hours the
revolution has been betrayed and you must raise the alarm; Who
has taken all the whisky from this cabinet? Why are you driving so
slowly? Why are you driving so fast? Tell me, Joe – do the people
love me? What do you think of this tie? Why are you smiling?
Why are you frowning? Joe, you are the only person I can trust;
Joe, my wife doesn't understand me; have a drink, Joe; Joe – I
know the working classes will never desert me, and I know you
love me – but, Joe: what are you really thinking?

By this time Joe was obviously a pretty confused man, but he
must have been clear enough in his mind to think: God get me out
of here and over to the Land of the Free, before this guy has me
shot for agreeing with him once too often.

And somehow, he managed it, this Joe, who also managed to
claim he was German as well as being a Hungarian Romanian.
And as he burbled out his story in that grimy passageway, he told
us how not so long ago he had returned to his village near
Timisoara, and greeted his old mother, and how at first his mother
hadn't recognized him, which nearly broke his heart.

Joe's bloodshot eyes were filling with tears and his gestures
became more and more histrionic as he told of the emotional
reunion with his family, and how he showered them all with magic
dollars. He was a bigshot back there, flown in for a few days from
the Home of the Brave. And now he unblocked drains and tied old
newspapers in bundles and put the garbage out, and lived in fear of
strangers, and terrorized unfamiliar faces, and had a half-starved
dog called – Joe. What other name was possible for this hound? I
tried to pat the thing but it nearly had my hand off. 'No – no –
don't ever try to touch him,' said the human Joe.

At this point, when the washer had long stopped rumbling in the
background, we heard a door creak open at the end of the passage,
and we saw a pale being approach us at a shuffle. It was a woman,
with pale blonde hair and bulbous blonde breasts and a face like a
ghost, emerging from the shadows, draped in a thin négligé, bags
under her sad eyes, sliding slowly towards us in a pair of purple

furry mules. This was Joe's daughter. She stopped still a good distance away, her bare white arms wrapped firmly around her fat torso. Like a bloated, careworn fish, she stared balefully at the three of us.

'Father,' she rapped out harshly. 'What are you doing?'

Her accent was uncorrupted by any signs of integration with the world above. Joe mumbled a few words of explanation. The girl was unmoved. Her face showed nothing but a weary contempt for all three of us.

'Crazy,' she said, tossed her head back, turned around, and shuffled away again, disappearing through the distant door from whence she had emerged, her glutinous flesh, untouched by natural light, wobbling as it went.

And shortly after this, the fat, sweaty superintendent Joe, and his familiar, the skinny canine namesake, hustled away after his daughter and left us to it to tumble dry our cottons and denims, and then to let the elevator whisk us back up to the light-filled apartment with its bare walls and stripped-clean floorboards and volumes of brand-new paperback literature: the Penguin dictionaries and Don DeLillo novels.

Before long Tom showed up, and we decided to drive down to the East Village to eat. Tom doesn't have a car, so we walked round the block to where ours was parked. As we approached it, an elderly gent came hurrying towards us from out of an apartment building: 'I think you should check your trunk,' he told us in a breathless French accent. It turned out that the previous night he'd seen some kid trying to force it open with a screwdriver, and had chased the boy off. Well, the lock was demonstrably looser, but it still worked, and inside the quart of oil and the coolers were inviolate, and the speakers we'd mounted under the rear shelf were still there. Looked like our good neighbour had done us a good turn. And it looked like he'd been waiting all day for us to show. But – nobody breaks into a bashed-up old car like this, do they? I've owned enough of them, God knows, and I knew that the lawless fraternity didn't waste its time on wrecks. Then I remembered Mary.

Mary was a slim, tight-jeaned, chainsmoking acquaintance of Richard and Judy who had visited one evening at Duck's Bottom and played Pictionary with us. She also talked non-stop about anything and everything – and let's just say it was on a somewhat more mundane level than one of Larry's after-dinner seminars. What we learned about Mary was that some months back she had been down at the coast, somewhere along the seventy-five-mile stretch of shoreline between Charleston and Myrtle Beach; and that along one deserted beach she had come across a recently wrecked light aeroplane. There was no sign of its pilot or passengers – but it still held its cargo, this being a substantial quantity of cocaine, which she promptly salvaged and made off with. Needless to say, in the period that followed she made much money and much whoopee with her fortuitous proceeds – which may have explained her fidgety disposition and the seriousness she attached to the most trivial transgressions of the laws of Pictionary. Now, whether or not the story about coming across the narcotics cargo by sheer accident was pure bullshit meant to cover up a more deliberate involvement is not of issue – the point is that planeloads of South American white stuff on South Carolinian shores are as common as runny noses in a kindergarten, and so a shabby car with SC plates in the middle of Manhattan probably stuck out like a neon sign to the average screwdriver-toting streetwise brother – a sign that read JUST SAY YO! TO THE VALUABLE SOUTH AMERICAN PLANT ALKALOIDS CONTAINED IN THIS TRUNK.

Nightlife in the East Village was as busy as ever – after dark it's one extended streetmarket, the sidewalks covered in second-hand books, clothing and bric-à-brac, their vendors more often than not overseeing their wares from the inside of a sleeping bag, else squatted on the front steps of their building, waiting for someone to buy a water pipe, a black velvet T-shirt, or a copy of *The Tin Drum* or *The Politics of Ecstasy*. The shops that stay open all night – little boutiques selling trendy clothing and contemporary paraphernalia – are clean and airy and have stripped floorboards, and they could be in Primrose Hill or the Left Bank; while the sidewalks are busy recycling the seventies, and the libraries of impoverished students. This is the unofficial campus of New York University, and it blends seamlessly with the city at large, the tourists, the homeless and the freaks. Tompkins Square Gardens had been surrounded by high chainlink fencing since I was last here, somewhat spoiling the view from the Odessa restaurant where we ate – according to Tom it was becoming too much of a needle park to tolerate. I munched on homely Hungarian cooking in this antique eaterie and remembered what a pleasant place the gardens had been – the basketball games, the chess players, the Life Café over the road ('Eat Life and Live'). But the old spectre of drug-related crimes and mayhem had apparently wiped out this scene.

Now this is the argument: if narcotics were to be legalized, and the state/community then supplied them and took responsibility for the users – bang goes your drug-related crime, and a person could get a fix in peace and indulge in an activity which victimizes no one except, arguably, the user. But to get anywhere near this idealistic scenario, government has to intervene; and America – especially right-wing America – is far too much in thrall to the questionable wisdom of that cracked old hippy on the pond, Henry David Thoreau, who has told them, 'That government is best, which governs least' (*Civil Disobedience,* 1849). And so it lets the banks take the drug profits and leaves everyone else to pick up the bloody pieces. Or leave them rotting on the street. I chewed on my sauerkraut and watched the walking wounded stumble by outside the window, and concluded that it was time Thoreau's ambiguous crap got dumped where it belonged, i.e. in a concrete canister at the bottom of Walden Pond. Some days later I was to find myself almost regretting this notion.

Next day we went out walking towards Central Park and, without even thinking about it, suddenly found ourselves in the lobby of the Metropolitan Museum of Art. What on earth were we doing here, we wondered, like sleepwalkers awaking. But now the question was: for a tourist of the mundane, did this place count as valid fare? A difficult one. The vast, hallowed vestibule echoed with ambiguous replies. We turned on our heels and left. Outside, some joker had put detergent into the fountain and the sidewalk was knee-deep in overflowing white froth. Japanese folk waded into it and gleefully took pictures of themselves. We took a walk around the park, where people dressed in tight, skimpy, black attire rushed past on roller blades. And in the evening we went by subway down to Greenwich Village and met up with Tom to go and eat at Sammy's, an airy, warehousy kind of place, full of more fashionable folk in black. I had black bean soup, which was fine, but funereal. I couldn't escape the feeling that young white New York was still mourning the loss of its presiding genius Warhol, and was freewheeling, waiting for the next surge of energy, from wherever it might come. At Sammy's we talked mainly of AIDS. Then we walked up through Times Square and over to the Plaza Hotel, where we ended the night in the dark recesses of the Oyster Bar with a long conversation about the psychology of suicide. August is a hot, sombre time in New York. Nobody really wants to be there.

You can always do without air-conditioning in a car, even in the most murderous heat, so long as you're moving reasonably fast. But Friday afternoon jams on the New England freeway don't allow this, and the hours of sluggish, sweaty progress it took to get a mere eighty miles and out beyond New Haven left us exhausted. It was even more tiresome, once off the interstate, to find no trace of a cheap motel in these rich green pastures around Guilford and Madison. This is where the continuous strip of coastal conurbation that stretches all the way out from New York City finally peters out into rural Connecticut, dotted with large secluded homesteads and neat-and-tidy timber toytown villages of white clapboard, preserved to an almost unreal degree by fierce planning regulations. In these places you have to look very hard indeed to spot a McDonalds, camouflaged and nestling discreetly in a row of sanitized shopfronts. A stark contrast to the anything-goes of the South: no giant billboards and mile-high illuminated signs around here: no junk, no funk, and no spunk. We fetched up for the night at the Dolly Madison Inne, a pricey little hotel by the sea. It reminded me of some of the more sterile watering holes along the waterways of South Devon: oafish men in Guernsey sweaters strutting about in their sea-captain fantasies and bullying the manageress, a young woman whose fixed smile looked to be giving her a great deal of pain. Bored middle-aged clientele sitting around the bar. I missed those rednecks. I gazed up at the TV and the inevitable baseball game. What was it about that game? As far as I knew it had never been played much in Germany – so what was so German about it? But the mystery remained.

Since our hotel bill allowed us use of the private beach, we rose early next morning and swam in the cool Atlantic, before heading off along the coast in search of a piece of ocean that wouldn't cost us anything. We should be so lucky. In this part of the world even the public beaches cost. Around lunch time we surrendered ten bucks to get into Hammonasset State Park, a wilderness dotted with pines and covered in tarmac, and fronted by a narrow sandy beach, complete with shower rooms, lifeguards and boardwalk. No commercial vulgarities are allowed in state parks and so this busy scene – families round their barbecues under the pines, the narrow strip of sand packed with sunbathers, and the boardwalk decorated with strolling tanned bodies – seemed unnaturally quiet and disciplined. It reminded me of pictures I'd seen of Soviet citizens holidaying at some Black Sea resort except that the citizens here were visibly better fed and more stylishly attired.

We found ourselves a spot on the sand and munched and lunched and observed our fellow leisure-seekers. The peculiar thing was that these people, tanned, healthy and nearly naked, should have been giving off some kind of erotic vibration, yet they were not. I stared at a girl lying nearby and wondered why I felt no twinge of sensual reaction whatsoever in circumstances which would normally produce anything from the least frisson of admiration to a definite swelling of spongy tissue. And it was soon clear that the same held for all these bodies, male or female: the muscular limbs, the shapely figures, the bronzed thighs; skipping down to the waves, walking back up the beach, sitting up to sip their drinks, turning over slowly to baste the other side of themselves – there was no electricity in the air, and the erotometer was firmly stuck on zero. And it wasn't just a matter of revealing-but-unsubtle clothing such as bollock-hugging briefs or luridly coloured bikinis: even the more sensual items of beachwear still failed to invest their owners with the slightest degree of sexuality.

Why was the air so devoid of such tension? Because the tension was all locked away in these folks' bodies. It was the way they held themselves and the way they moved. Every pose they made, and every step they took was a denial of what all this healthy flesh actually meant. There was a rigidity about the men, and a cautiousness about the women. No languidity or lissomness here: the well-developed shoulders, the strong thighs, the firm tits – none of this flesh was being allowed to flow or ripple. Everything was held back. It was a revealing exhibition of the contradictory alliance between body-culture and sexual repression. It made for a landscape of android-like creatures who seemed to be equipped with everything but that final breath of essential reproductive spirit.

This tight, bound way in which so many Americans carry themselves can be noticed everywhere, it's just more starkly obvious on a beach. Theirs is, after all, a very military and religious culture, where every indigenous-born adult has spent every morning of their schooldays reciting the oath of allegiance: One Nation Under God, and so on -- which amounts to more than two thousand mornings at attention beneath the flag. That's a fair old bit of conditioning by any standard, and perhaps it explains why so many of them feel insecure without Old Glory hanging in their front yard.

Or on their bumpers and meat hats: there were plenty of these on view along Highways 77 and 19 as we took the fifty-mile drive north to Hartford that afternoon through the green and pleasant stuff. And, as elsewhere, plenty of trees tied with yellow ribbons, which showed that there were plenty of hostages, soldiers, and missing children yet to return home. In Hartford itself our route should have taken us past the state capitol, but this was blocked by police lines which forced us on a long detour through the grimmer parts of town, the run-down black and hispanic quarters, before we finally located the street we were looking for, a slightly more upmarket street in the middle of all this seedy geography. We pulled into the driveway of a smallish two-storey house of white clapboard, walked round the back, noting its spacious garden, and rapped on the kitchen door. After a moment this door opened, and I was surprised to find myself staring at the tall figure of tennis star Boris Becker.

It wasn't, of course, but I took some convincing, because this man was the spitting image of the famous German. His real name was Ed Bauer, an acquaintance of Rosey's from ten years back when they had met at a Swiss ski resort while working at the same restaurant/nightclub. Ed had been the bouncer, and it showed. The guy was enormous. His wife Jenny, a dark, tight-lipped woman, was equally tall. And they had a long-limbed, blond-haired and blue-eyed four-year-old kid called Rolf, a shy little boy who immediately rushed off to go play in something he called a 'sin box'. I later discovered that this was in fact a sand box, but that Rolf spoke the word like a southern preacher would say 'sinned'. So he ran out to the yard, and Ed pulled out beers from the fridge and swiftly barbecued up some hefty salmon steaks on the porch grill. And after we'd consumed these, first Bill and then Gail turned up, both bearing six-packs. Bill, in shorts and penny loafers, said he worked in insurance but he wasn't too happy about his future. Hartford billed itself as the Insurance Capital of the World, but as he pointed out (and as the next day's papers did too, so it happened), nobody can afford insurance any more. Gail, bespectacled, talkative and Jewish, was still in her working clothes – she travelled in laboratory equipment, but she was looking to change her career. Fine time to do that, was the general opinion. Jenny worked for IBM, and she was also feeling insecure – they were already laying off people. The difference about this recession was that white collar workers weren't safe any longer. Ed himself, who had been in real estate, had recently been out of work for a year; he now worked for a church-run housing association, constructing basic accommodation with volunteer labour. These people – as ordinary Americans as you're likely to meet – were clearly worried folks, and plenty of folks they knew were currently unemployed.

Gail revealed the reason why we had earlier been diverted from our route via the state capitol – Jesse Jackson, on a 'crusade' through Connecticut, had held a rally there that afternoon, and Gail had been at it. According to her, Jackson was the only person telling it like it is on the issues that mattered – health care, housing, education, unemployment – and was calling for more government involvement and more public spending. No other Democrat was standing up to be counted. And nobody disagreed with her around this table. Jackson would get their vote anytime. Trouble was he wasn't standing. And there was nobody else in sight. Result: intense pessimism round the table. This wasn't lifted when the subject turned to cats. Gail was a 'cat person'. She had a lot of them, and they were costing her fortunes in veterinary bills. 'Every examination costs me two hundred bucks,' she complained. Myself, I couldn't imagine busting my wallet over a beast – would they do the same for me? I'm afraid that if I had a cat that got sick I would let it live or die by its own fortune, I stated as clearly as five cans of Coors would let me. This heartless, Republican attitude towards health care was politely ignored.

Next day being Sunday, the Bauers were off on family business, and we two tourists took a tour of Hartford. It was grim. The deserted downtown was criss-crossed by overhead freeways. In the park by the Connecticut River we watched scores of men taking to the water in what appeared to be some kind of competition to see who could best emulate the George-Bush-At-Kennebunkport image, each with meat hat, crate of beer and twenty-seven different fishing rods sticking up from the prow of their craft. But elsewhere in that humid, wasp-ridden park, a most bizarre sight: a game of cricket, on a proper cricket field, with pavilion, boundary markers and everyone dressed in immaculate whites. Hartford's West Indian community hard at it, and playing to a high standard, what's more. 'Jorry good show,' I cried, my mouth full of corn chips and salsa sauce, applauding each boundary shot. There was hope yet for America.

But this wasn't what tourists come to see in Hartford. So we took ourselves off to where we should have been, to the more genteel, west side of the city, the leafy trees, the nineteenth-century houses with their broad front lawns. Here, slap bang next to each other, were the Mark Twain and Harriet Beecher-Stowe residences, preserved for posterity. In an outbuilding which served as a visitors' centre for both houses we discovered that posterity would have to pay bucks to enter and be led around these domiciles, and moreover we'd have to wait half an hour for the next guided walkabout. So instead we checked out the postcards in the gift shop and gained a pretty comprehensive idea of how Twain and Stowe had lived. Extravagantly was the answer. The interiors were palatial, the furnishings sumptuous, the joinery positively baroque. It was a great little tour and the views were unobstructed. Later on, over doorstep steaks at the Bauers, we were easily able to pretend we'd done the actual traipse. We feared they'd otherwise have been offended, since they had sincerely recommended the tour. They nodded in recognition as we described items in loving detail: 'We saw those carvings too!' said Jenny.

'On the postcards,' said Ed. 'We didn't actually do the tour.'

We'd gone native without realizing it.

Jenny and Ed (who first met ten years back in Ed's home town of Casenovia, NY) were eager to tell us about their lives in fine socio-psychological detail. Thus we learned about Jenny's 'dysfunctional' family and its sordid history; and of a certain incident whose shadow was still cast over the household – when a year or so ago one of Jenny's sleazy uncles was supposed to have molested the child Rolf whilst babysitting. The repercussions of this event helped explain the boy's clear distrust of me, in contrast to his complete acceptance of Rosey. Ed had obviously given him some severe warnings about the men of the planet. But eventually Rolf accepted me as a bone-fide chum and went so far as to allow me to play with him in the sin box; and before we left I was even to get to bathe the pale little mite, though I must confess that I didn't know where to look when, during the course of this event, he climbed on to the lavatory seat and started to frig himself during the process of his business – but the problem was, his little doubled-up body was already halfway down the pan, and he was far too busy with himself to notice this. Not wanting to approach him for fear of starting rumours, I stepped outside the bathroom and monitored him through the keyhole to make sure he didn't drop any further during the course of his preoccupation, or worse, flush himself entirely away. But eventually he hauled himself out, and once his stem was back to normal I resumed my caring duties.

The Monday morning after our vicarious trip around Auntie Harriet and Uncle Mark's respective cabins, we were awoken early in our sleep-sofa in the living room to learn of another person who was very nearly down the pan. Ed shook us awake, pressed mugs of coffee into our hands. 'Well, folks,' he said with the tone of someone trying desperately to sound cheerful, 'the news this morning is that, firstly, there's a hurricane approaching, and if that's not bad enough, there's been a coup in Russia and Gorbachev's under house arrest. Do you realize what this means?'

What it meant to me was that suddenly the world was a good deal less safe, hurricane or not. And what it meant to Ed was equally clear: 'Do you *know* how much this'll wipe off the stock exchange?' he declared, as he switched on the TV and the news began to burble out.

We spent the rest of the morning bringing stuff in from the garden and stashing it in the cellar – bicycles, BBQ grills, chairs,

tables, toys, junk – anything that moved – and grimly battening
down the hatches. It was bizarre – was this for the hurricane, or
the nuclear war, or both? One thing that it meant for sure: more
publicity for speedboats, fishing rods and meat hats, because just
as when the Gulf crisis broke, the Presnightstates was currently on
vaction, pootling about off the coast of Maine. Since Hurricane
Bob was scheduled to be shortly doing the same, it didn't seem
such a bad thing.

But Hurricane Bob only side-swiped Hartford and brought a
few trees and power lines down, and in a couple of days
Gorbachev was back in the Kremlin. A certain town in Michigan
was quick off the mark, as we saw on Wednesday's TV news:
they had erected a huge billboard which read WELCOME BACK GORBY
– NEXT TIME VACATION IN MICHIGAN!

Although Ed and Jenny didn't watch much TV (Rolf was the
main consumer – he spent five evenings in a row in front of the
Sesame Street Christmas Show videotape), something told me they
were probably *Roseanne* fans. Weren't this show's heroes
supposed to be Mr and Mrs ordinary working-class America,
battling bravely to keep their friendly, unpretentious lifestyle going
against all the slings and arrows?

'Oh, sure,' said Jenny, 'I always try to watch that show. Even
though they say such nasty things to each other.'

Nasty things? And I thought it was all rumbustuous jokery. But
it figured. There was something brittle in the atmosphere at the
Bauers which didn't tolerate exchanges of the leg-pulling variety.
Conversations were pretty serious most of the time, and
expressions of affection tended to be of the reassuring kind. Piss-
taking was out in this household. There was too much vulnerability
in the air. Jenny was only too happy to admit that she was only
now, at thirty-three, beginning to accumulate some self-esteem,
after a childhood at odds with her alcoholic father and many sad
affairs until she'd met Ed; and it had taken five years of marriage
and then finally a child for her self-confidence to start to flow. Ed,
it appeared, was always the stable partner, always the support-
supplier, and it was clear that he was still actively committed to
this role. Most of what he said to her was in the nature of
reassurance, telling her she was good enough to do X, Y or Z at
work, she was right to tell her rotten brother this or that, that she

looked good, that he loved her, and so on – in the laundry/
workshop/basement was a large painted message across one wall:
I LOVE YOU JENNY. But I could see that Ed's self-appointed all-
supportive role would make him weary at the end of a long day,
especially since he took so much time in reassuring his son, too: I
lost count of the number of times the kid would be told he was
loved; maybe this was to counterbalance the extremely strict
routines Rolf was put through by his father at the dining table, in
the bathroom, and all the other domestic routines a child goes
through – this was in contrast to Jenny's more *laissez-faire*
approach. So for every harsh father's word, Ed would follow up
with a series of 'I-Love-You's that bordered on the overwhelming.
It was clear that Ed was finding fatherhood hard work, and this
complete separation of discipline from affection – the two could
never come together in the same moment – may only have been
confusing the kid. Jokes and leg-pulls, which rely on contradiction,
are paradoxically reassuring vehicles – in fact they're positively
cosy, which is why they're the stuff of domestic sitcoms like
Married with Children or *Roseanne*, where everybody loves each
other really, despite all those 'nasty things' they say. The business
of loving was harder work with the Bauers.

The days he wasn't working for Habitats For Humanity, Ed ran
his own small carpentry and decorating business, and I helped him
out here for a couple of days, while Rosey minded the kid at home.
Rolf normally went to the Waldorf/Steiner school in West
Hartford, but he was suffering from an insect bite which had made
his eye swell up like a boxer's. He loved to dress up, and he got
Rosey to help make him a papier mâché crown – a *queen's* crown,
he insisted. He was a very sensual boy and he liked improvising
skirts from bits of material, and making himself necklaces and
bracelets from things like paper clips. Jenny appreciated her son's
creativity, but she said she had 'drawn the line' recently when, in
Woolworths, he'd asked her to buy him a bunch of coloured
ribbons. And Ed was heard one breakfast time whispering
earnestly to the kid that he must have a *king's* crown because girls
and boys were different. Rolf had an interesting life ahead of him.

By Thursday, despite the Bauers' protestations, we were ready
to move on. Things were becoming a little *too* mundane. Besides, I
had a feeling we had contributed to the slightly haggard look that

Ed had developed – too many after-midnights with him once Jenny was abed, when he'd break out the bourbon and marijuana around the kitchen table; another surreptitious toker.

It was time to go west. We reckoned on six days to reach the Rockies and Denver, and another four to travel up through Wyoming and Montana and thence into northern Idaho near the Canadian border, where we'd been offered hospitality by another couple Rosey had met during the time she'd spent in Switzerland – here we would have a place to holiday awhile among the mountains and lakes of the north-western Rockies. Between here and there was about three and a half thousand miles of non-stop interstate. We set off out of Hartford south-west on I-84 towards the New York state line. Once across this the road surface deteriorated considerably – overused and underfunded – but the scenery was tremendous as we hit the Appalachians in all their glorious greenery: up mountain and down valley, across the Croton, the Taconic Parkway, and over the wide Hudson River between Beacon and Newburgh. It was shortly after this that we pulled into a rest area, and as I changed down through the gears I realized something was very wrong: in order not to crash the gears I was having to force the clutch pedal right down to the floor. We rolled to a halt and checked as much as we could in our ignorance – i.e. the fluid level in the clutch reservoir, which seemed OK. Then we took turns to crawl under the car while the other worked the clutch pedal. There was a mechanism of rods pushing back and forth into a cylinder, with nothing apparently broken or dripping. Well ... maybe the trouble would just sort of go away? We drove the car slowly up and down the parking area to see if it would and to check I wasn't just imagining all this. It wouldn't and I wasn't. We should find a garage. So where were we, and where was the nearest town? We consulted the map. The nearest town was just a couple of miles north of the interstate. A little place called Walden. Wait a minute – Walden? *The* Walden? This was beginning to look suspiciously like Thoreau's revenge.

3. A Favour for Limon

I'd asked for it, really. First to insult the revered philosopher, and then to pass within spitting distance of his old haunt, making it only too easy for his ghost to reach out and undo me. But I still held out hope that Thoreau's shade might not be that malevolent, and had merely decided to create a temporary glitch. Perhaps if we just left the car alone for a while, it would right itself – surely old Henry David would approve of that? And if we could just get far enough away from Walden, and out of his sphere of influence ... so we waited for a while, had a smoke and a drink, and then reboarded the Datsun to see if we would be able to escape this haunted vicinity.

And happily now, the clutch seemed to be working as I pulled away and shifted up through the gears till we were back on the highway and fast leaving Walden behind us. We were soon in Pennsylvania, and it was sylvan alright. The deeper we penetrated into the Appalachians, the more spectacular it became. The interstate had become considerably less busy, and it was the most enlightening place from which to view the great swathes of forest and lakeland, since it was generally unhindered by the blinkering, claustrophobic effect of tall lines of trees planted close to the verge that they went in for down South. We crossed the Pocono Mountains and joined I-81 at Scranton, and then rolled down to the Susquehanna valley, with twenty miles of the Scranton/Wilkes-Barre conurbation on our right; and as this petered out we pulled into a truck stop for refreshment. Here we found the classic American diner, a dying phenomenon these days as truck stops get bigger and their restaurants tend to be giant brick-built barns. But this was the full step-up-to-it stainless steel longhouse, quiet, clean, air-conditioned, with young, efficient waitresses and good quality cheap food. I should say inexpensive food. 'Cheap' to an

American means tawdry; ask for directions to cheap
accommodation or cheap food and you'll find yourself at some
sleaze pit. The best basic food in all truck stops is an inexpensive,
large bowl of chilli with all the saltine crackers you can eat,
followed by as many cups of coffee as you need to get your
money's worth of caffeine (this usually works out at about four
cups). And the best thing about truck stop diners is that the air
remains quietly unpolluted by the collective neuroses of those who
frequent fancier restaurants or the lurid fast-food palaces. There's
no fuss at a truck stop, and none of that phoney eager-to-please-
you business. They function better, and they're ch– less expensive.

From here we climbed away up into the Penobscots and then
joined I-80, which would eventually take us all the way to Ohio.
By evening we had descended once again to the Susquehanna, and
after crossing it near Mifflinville we left the interstate and joined
Highway 11, which runs parallel, and which took us into the
pleasant college town of Bloomsburg as night fell and we searched
for a motel. Ten miles further on we pulled into the Stone Castle
on an empty stretch near Danville. There was nothing lapidary or
castellian about it, however – it was the usual terrace of rooms –
unless you count the way its overdressed, middle-aged manageress
had decorated her large office – *à l'Espagnol* it was, the walls
hung with vivid red tapestries depicting bullfights, and every
available surface supporting figurines of matadors and
banderilla'd bulls. 'I just love Spain,' she told us, and even
claimed – with little commitment in her voice – that she hoped to
visit it one day. Our room's colour scheme was also scarlet and, to
be fair, above the electric fire was a fake chimney of stone-like
plastic tiles. We hit the air-conditioning and flopped out. I tried the
TV: only five channels – four were running commercials at that
moment, and on the fifth was an *I Love Lucy* rerun. I needed a
drink. I decided to drive back to Bloomsburg and find a liquor
store.

But I couldn't get the car into gear. The Curse of Thoreau had
struck again, with a vengeance.

The next morning we managed to nurse the sick vehicle back
into Bloomsburg, and while the local foreign car specialist looked
it over he lent us a Volvo to get up to the truck stop on the
interstate to have breakfast. The place was a brick-built barn

number which sold charming postcards of 'Strip Mining in Pennsylvania' – photos of a mechanical excavator sitting in a quarry; and different aerial views of this place, 'Buckhorn Truckstop on Interstate 80, PA'. These pictures elevated the banal to stunning new mid-levels. I hadn't seen anything like them since Richard Ffarington had sent me a postcard of a nondescript traffic roundabout in the city centre of Sheffield, England. I bought a couple of these ones with which to return the compliment.

Our Bloomsburg man told us, standing in his yard full of MGs, Volvos and a solitary old Morris Marina (!), that we needed a new clutch cylinder, and that if we could get ourselves another twenty miles along the road to Susquehanna Valley Nissan they'd put it in for us right away. So we limped along to the highway at Hummel's Wharf with its reassuring vista of wall-to-wall dealerships, located Nissan, and were told they'd have the car fixed in an hour. Hummel's Wharf – A Nice Place To Break Down In, that's what the town sign should have read. A place where mechanics look you in the eye. But this is true of the country as a whole. I've never encountered the sleazy, quasi-pornographic atmosphere you get in so many British repair shops, those smutty businesses which seek to hide behind the anonymity of initials – 'M. T. Gearboxes', 'F. U. Motors', etc. – and whose evasiveness always smacks of deceit. This might be because your average American is more mechanically minded and knows enough about his or her car to discourage bullshitting and mystification.

The weather was hot and sultry. We walked across a couple more dealership lots to the Dairy Queen kiosk and cooled off with water-ices. Dairy Queens are an institution, one of the first fast-food chains, begun in the 1920s. For all I knew this one was seventy years old, a landmark, an antique, a piece of local heritage, sitting at the corner of the highway and a small road leading uphill to a residential settlement. How many folks had been directed to turn off at the Dairy Queen, had worked their way through studies there, fallen in love beneath its red-and-white sign, given back their eternity pin there, smashed Mom's car there, been there the day Kennedy was shot? In fact residential Hummel's Wharf turned out to be a large chunk of heritage itself: a collection of modest, mostly weatherboarded houses in a little grid of neat-

and-tidy streets, their hedgeless lawns running to the road's edge,
and in a number of driveways a pastel-coloured fifties' sedan – not
your ostentatious big Chevy or Cadillac restored by an enthusiast
and driven for fun and show, but smaller four-cylinder Fords and
Chryslers, immaculately preserved, looking like they had been in
everyday use since the end of the Korean War. The house, the
lawn, the car: together in an icon of thrifty, temperate middle-
American aspirations, but here curiously backdated. There were
no satellite dishes on view to go with the flags and basketball
hoops. It looked like the land from where Schultz first sprung
Peanuts on the world: there was Snoopy's white kennel, and there
on the doorstep lay the brown carapace of a baseball mitt. The
scene could have served equally well as a backdrop for the *Denis
The Menace* cartoons – not the British Dennis, not the spiky-haired
punk-desperado, but America's 'lovable' scamp, a blond puppy-
in-dungarees whom I judged wimpy in 1957 and who appears
nowadays in newspapers in single-frame adventures which usually
consist of cute, childish questions demanded of his exasperated-
yet-adoring Mom. Compare these two trickster-figures – the one
brutal, Celtic, streetwise, a bully with a pit-bull factotum; the other
belonging firmly in some kindergarten or *Barnehage*, infinitely
more sanitized, only a few hairs out of place on his angelic head,
only a tiny catapult for weaponry. The British Dennis would end
an adventure with dirt on his face; the American Denis would
finish with Mom cleaning the dirt *off* his face – clearly a diluted
version of which Bruno Bettelheim would not approve. This may
tell us something about the two nations; on the other hand America
does far better when it comes to animals as tricksters – Bugs
Bunny being the prime example – whereas there are no enduring
British versions. The country that produced the RSPCA could not
be expected to come up with anything approaching the savage,
cathartic violence of *Tom & Jerry* or *Roadrunner*. But America is
always closer to the wild and rural origins of this style of story-
telling, and all these cartoon creatures that come out of Hollywood
(itself a creature founded by central Europeans) – the bears, deer,
skunks, raccoons, coyotes, alleycats, vultures, Southern Rats and
so forth, are still part of the landscape, whether robbing trashcans,
fooling park rangers and policemen, chewing an old car to pieces
or lying dead on the highway. A Grimm's America, especially

here in the pine forests; and perhaps, too, some of the animism of the native Americans has seeped into the general consciousness.

By mid-afternoon, with the vehicle fixed and a hundred bucks poorer, we were rolling again. What more can I say about the beauty of the Alleghenies? Not much. They're pleasant to drive through, and they allow you to think and talk about whatever you like without being too distracting, because one ten-mile stretch of I-80 is pretty much like the next, and the next. That's the thing about stunning beauty, it leaves you clobbered numb after a while. And there were lots of dead, truck-clobbered deer, too, and along the lesser highway we took towards the end of the day, as the mountains turned to foothills, for fifty miles we saw a NO TOXIC WASTE DUMP HERE sign in every garden of every home in every community, from Cranberry to Pecan, from Cherry Valley to Nectarine.

We finished up at the more prosaic town of Farrel, a mile or so from the Ohio line, and stopped at the 7-Up motel. The manageress, a middle-aged white-permed woman, looked at us suspiciously at first from behind her locked screen door. It was clear she didn't want her place used as a knocking shop, unlike our hostess of the previous night, who (so we'd been informed back in Bloomsburg) was running a pretty successful bordello at the Stone Castle, where client met girl at the bar across the highway also owned by Madame – she was making enough out of her business to run her own plane from her own airstrip behind the motel. The 7-Up manageress eventually unlocked her door and took our respectable money. 'End room,' she said tersely, locked up again and was gone. This motel really was small – not even a Pepsi machine. Inside our tiny room we gasped for breath, rushed to turn on the air-conditioner, crushed a few cockroaches, turned on the black-and-white TV, then pulled various supermarket delicacies from our cooler and picnicked before retiring.

The Midwest began abruptly early the next morning, as soon as we crossed the Ohio line near Youngstown. The previous day the road had been winding and mountainous; now it was straight and flat. Yesterday all views had been green; now they were all bleached-brown – a million acres of ripening corn, each field with its own little oil pump bobbing up and down like a heat-crazed donkey beating its head against the ground. Mid-morning we encountered a free coffee stall at a rest area: a little trailer run by a local church group. The coffee was the weakest we'd tasted yet, and it was only free if your conscience was clear about not making a contribution to their funds. Ours was.

My fondest memory of Ohio is something which was actually a distraction from Ohio: a wacky little show on National Public Radio entitled *Car Talk*, which features two jolly male Bostonians who sound as if they are broadcasting from a corner of *Cheers*. They take phone-in questions on mechanical problems, anti-rust treatments, mysterious noises and quirks, and everything else to do with man's best friend. And so you get exchanges like: 'Uh, hi, yes, my name is Elmer and I'm from Sump, Michigan, and I want to know what I should do with my '75 Charger –'

'Get rid of it, Elmer!' the boys respond in unison.

'I was going to say,' Elmer ploughs on doggedly, 'that's losing the chrome bits around the ashtray ...'

'Answer's the same, Elmer – get rid of it!'

'Nah, he's only joking. The answer is: quit smoking! Though on balance I'd say a '75 Charger is worse for your health –'

' – and your bank account. Bye Elmer and thanks for calling *Car Talk*. Do we have another caller?'

'Hi, I'm Rachael? From Athens, Georgia? I have a Fiat 128?'

'You have a *Fiat 128*?!'

(sustained laughter for a minute or so until the boys regain their composure)

And so on. Americans talking about their cars. Big cars, small cars, and lots of payment-overdue cars. But I don't remember a single problem with a Japanese car.

Meanwhile, ours was rolling ever onwards, through what Ohio license plates call 'The Heart Of It All'.

Two hundred singularly unenlightened miles later we crossed into Indiana. Indiana was grey, overcast and sticky, and it had a lot of racetracks and cornfields. In one of these, curiously situated directly behind a thirty-foot-high Shellgas billboard, was a cluster of three twenty-foot high timber crucifixes, the two outer ones painted blue and the central cross taller and painted gold. This was undoubtedly the work of Bernard Coffindaffer, one of America's more remarkable contemporary environmental artists.

Coffindaffer's story begins in World War II, when he was a young soldier out in the Pacific, involved in the battle for Guadalcanal, where on one occasion his company tried unsuccessfully to take a hill from the Japanese. Coffindaffer was badly injured in the failed assault, and whilst recovering in hospital he received a vision. It was an angel of the Lord, announcing that he, Bernard Coffindaffer, had been chosen by God on high to carry out, in B.C.'s words, 'the greatest mission since Saint Paul's'. What the Lord wanted, it transpired, was an America where every hill and dale would be marked by a clear reminder of His Son's suffering and death at Calvary. But – young Bernard was not to begin his task right away. He must go back home, and work, and make money. The Lord would eventually let him know when the time was ripe. And this is indeed what the Lord did, although it was some forty working years later. Coffindaffer, having finally amassed his capital, now hired a handful of men in a couple of pick-ups and set them about their work. They started in the South in the early eighties. Coffindaffer would inspect the countryside, find an imposing bluff or an attractive little meadow, then seek out the landowner and inform the person that he, Bernard Coffindaffer, was 'seizing the spot for Jesus of Nazareth', and he hoped the owner would not be foolish enough to object. And nine times out of ten the owner didn't. This was a particularly God-fearing part of the country, after all.

I saw my first Coffindaffer cluster in the middle of a meadow in Transylvania County, North Carolina, in 1988. Since it was Easter time I assumed the crosses had been erected for Holy Week and would shortly be dismantled. Else it was some local custom supposed to keep vampires away. Not so. Travelling around the South over the next couple of months I saw these things everywhere, from Virginia to Mississippi, in cornfields, meadows, on hilltops and riverbanks. Coffindaffer had about ten teams working for him by now, and they had put up around a thousand of these diverting *memento moris* the length and breadth of Dixieland. There were some people who objected to all of this – local journalists and others – and there were some who took direct action and destroyed his work with a few swift strokes of a chainsaw. Coffindaffer's response was not particularly gracious. On one occasion Christianity's answer to Christo claimed to be on

excellent terms with a number of county sheriffs, who had told
him that they would be happy to personally take a chainsaw to the
limbs of anybody they found trying to destroy 'God's work'.
Coffindaffer also claimed the support of those such as Jerry
Falwell, who had praised him in person, and the Pope of Rome,
whose blessings had arrived on the hearsay of an American
cardinal. So now the young man who had failed to take a hill for
the US Marines had realized a good part of his pentathol-induced
vision and had conquered patches of ground the length and
breadth of the south-eastern United States. Returning this year I
had been curious to see how the project was going, and was
intrigued to have spotted no sign of Coffindaffer's crosses
anywhere east of the Appalachians. Was his mission failing, then?
Or had I simply not seen enough of the country? But here now in
Indiana was a sign that the man was moving west. A strange spot
to choose, however: directly behind an effacing billboard, barely
visible. Maybe it was some statement about the reverse side of
worldly commerce. More likely, though, the farmer had said, 'You
can put up your crosses here so long as they don't get in the way
of my tractor.' Not long after this sighting, we saw another – this
time a solitary blue cross, bereft of its companions, close to the
road. Coffindaffer was clearly finding it tougher going as he
blazed his trail west.

We were pretty exhausted ourselves by the end of that day as
we came into Brazil, a small town in the far west of the state.
Rosey was that tired she ran a red light on Main Street, and we
were promptly pulled over by a cop. As we made to leave our
vehicle we were quickly put back in our seats by the nervous shout
of 'STAY IN THE CAR! STAY IN THE CAR!', so familiar from
a thousand movie dramas. Looked at from the cop's point of view,
we may well have been armed desperados, in our shabby car with
out-of-state plates – especially South Carolinian ones, which must
stick out a mile. (South Carolinians rarely drive more than a few
miles beyond their own borders; the same isn't true for Georgians
and Floridians, for example, whose plates we saw everywhere,
from coast to coast; but in all our trip we didn't see a single other
SC license, and we were told by more than one person that ours
was the first they had ever seen. Then again, there are so many
Americans who know little of their own country save perhaps the

adjoining two or three states. Even those who have travelled widely in Europe and elsewhere will confess to knowing little of the greater US.)

'I don't wanna grouch or nothin',' said the young cop deferentially, 'but you *did* go through that red light.' He was impressed and bemused by our international licenses, old-fashioned booklets with pages and pages in Arabic, Cyrillic, and other exotic scripts, which resembled ambassadors' credentials. We were the first British he'd ever met, and he couldn't imagine why we had bothered to come to Brazil, Indiana. When we asked him the whereabouts of an inexpensive motel he squirmed a little and then directed us ten miles up the road to Terre Haute, when he said there'd be plenty of Budget Hosts, Holiday Inns and so forth. But surely Brazil itself had a little place of its own somewhere? For some reason our cop was reluctant to admit it but he finally gave us directions to the Villa Motel across town; and then went off without booking us.

The Villa was another thirty-year-old establishment on the edge of a highway whose traffic had been all but stolen by the interstate. The manageress was another bleached-and-permed woman, but a good deal friendlier than the proprietrix of the 7-Up. I commented on the unusually early checkout time of 10 a.m. 'Oh, don't worry about that,' she replied. 'We only have that because the locals like to use the rooms and they'd otherwise be inclined to hang around all morning.' Well now, what could this mean? The Villa – The Stone Castle: a secure, almost besieged ring about both names.

Next morning around eight we were awakened by some of the aforementioned locals getting in as much activity as possible before checkout. Through the paper-thin wall it came loud and clear – two young women and a stud called Brad. 'Oh Brad, I don't know where you git your energy from ...' – 'I'm gonna lie on my front – just massage my back awhile ...' – 'Brad, I'm trying to watch TV for goodness sakes ...' Later on we saw them leave – three young folks dressed up like country musicians in 'cowboy' gear, zooming off in a gleaming new pick-up, doubtless keen to get to church on time this Sunday morning. Before we two also left, we treated ourselves to a drink made from the complimentary sachets of brown powder and non-dairy creamer; yes, we had an awful cup of coffee in Brazil.

We ourselves got to church on time in St Louis, after racing through the corn-covered flat horizons of southern Illinois in 96 degree heat, stopping periodically at the rest centres and saturating ourselves with cold showers under the lawn sprinklers. We were just in time for 3 o'clock mass in the French Cathedral, on the south bank of the Mississippi. An unusually airy and uncluttered building for a Catholic cathedral. The celebrant priest opened proceedings with a speech from the pulpit delivered in appallingly incompetent French. He was attempting to explain what relevance King Louis XII, the cathedral's dedicatee, had for us today. It seemed to hinge on the fact that Louis had twelve children – 'dooze on fontz' – and the congregation was being subtly invited to emulate him. Since the cathedral was full of families who were already way ahead of Louis the King, the sermon seemed a singular waste of words. We left before the wine and biscuits. Nearby, we admired a hundred-foot-high structure of stainless steel which appeared to be one half of the McDonald's 'M', but in fact turned out to be 'The Gateway To The West', a celebration of St Louis' role during the pioneering days. Down on the conspicuously uncrowded waterfront a couple of shabby old tourist riverboats were not doing much business. We drove out through the derelict docklands and rejoined I-70, and were in Columbia by evening, where we could find nothing but a barrack-like Budget Host Inn to put us up. In the room lay a little note from the chamberperson bidding us welcome and hoping we'd enjoy our stay and appreciate the cleanliness of the room. An unsubtle demand for a tip from someone we were unlikely even to clap eyes on. The room was clean alright, but I had to sleep with earplugs for the noise of the adjacent interstate. In the morning we claimed our free breakfast of weak coffee and cinnamon doughnut down in the lobby and were gone by eight.

By noon we were through both Kansas Cities and were pulling into the Kansas state welcome center. Every state has one of these at its main points of entry. They'll usually give you coffee, maps, information about accommodation; and more often than not suggest you visit the trolley museum in some little town called Emporia or Glendale. The Kansas maps made a point of showing all the different frontier trails that once crossed the state, and suggesting we go and look for the ruts. Twenty miles into the state it was clear that the West had begun, as traffic thinned to a minuscule flow and gas stations and food stops were now few and far between. Passing close by the old frontier town of Lawrence, from where so many pioneers set off in the middle of the last century for the Rockies and beyond, I saluted in its direction, just in case that old literary pioneer Mr William S. Burroughs should happen to be at home there, perhaps sitting on his porch shooting at the birds on the telephone wire, or maybe just staring out towards his beloved Western Lands and meditating on space travel. I imagined that one day folk like us might breeze through Lawrence and visit the Burroughs shack, forgo the guided tour, and settle for a few enlightening postcards of its hallowed interior.

Fifty miles west of Topeka, where the flint hills descend towards the Kansas River, we were given a splendid view of the Fort Riley military camp, where a vast compound was chock full of vehicles recently returned from the Gulf War: endless rows of trucks, tankers and jeeps bearing the coalition's single chevron and wearing that grubbied-up desert camouflage so familiar from TV. At nearby Junction City they were glad to have the soldiers home. All the banks and commercial premises still bore large banners in support of their troops, while improvised notices on the doors of the bars and niteries welcomed the boys back. Junction City, a town of fewer than two thousand inhabitants, had a disproportionately large number of clubs and bars on account of the military, who were everywhere in their green fatigues and meat hats – dumping great sacks of donations at the thrift shop or loading up six trolleys each at the supermarket. We spent a few hours wandering about an otherwise most normal American town, visiting cafés, drugstores, thrift shops, the post office, the supermarkets, marvelling at Junction City's placid, archaic mundanity. But even in a small place like this, where most of the commerce takes place on just a few downtown blocks, we saw nobody on the sidewalks. It bore the look of a ghost town filled only with cars. From the street you might catch a brief glimpse of somebody crossing the sidewalk from car to shop or back again, but apart from this it looked deceptively empty. Nobody walks so much as a block in towns like this. Nobody except mad English folk like us, out in the fierce heat, feeling extremely conspicuous. It's a strange sensation to step from an empty sidewalk into a crowded bank or busy post office, and then out again and into a shimmering silence broken only by the burbling of the odd automobile. And the cars themselves move slowly, quietly, unhurriedly, all over rural America. Nobody rushes and roars like the blue-arsed Brits or the frenetic French. It gives this nation a strangely peaceful appearance.

After leaving Junction City we took fifty miles of ancient highway through even smaller towns where all but the few modern cars and trucks produced an even more emphatic suggestion of the 1950s. And when some old fellow steps down from a '54 pick-up in his dungarees and meat hat, and spits out a wad of tobacco before hobbling across to a general store whose sign was put up long before the last war, you expect to hear a director shouting 'Cut!'

There is more of the immediate past preserved here than you'll ever see in Western Europe, and it can be much more poignant than a castle or a suit of armour, if only because it has been a part of one's own time. I'm not American, and I couldn't have been brought up further away from, say, Bavaria, Kansas, but all the same I watched TV and went to Saturday morning pictures and read the glossy-covered comic mags; and the long cars with their whitewall tyres, and the Rexall drugstores, and all the accoutrements of small-town America were part of my vicarious experience. They were the backdrop for countless episodes of *Mr Ed, Highway Patrol* and the rest. And while few signs of my childhood survive at home save the basic outlines of streets and buildings, in the US there is a significant chunk of it uncannily preserved, and in three dimensions what's more. There is simply no comparison with rural England, where nobody but a collector drives fifties' cars or trucks, nobody dresses in the same backdated way – Britain's island suburb people are desperate to cover their tracks, to redesign their environment and their identity; there's no time and no space to stand still. But here I was stepping into scenes I had first absorbed as a four-year-old, from the pages of my first reading book. And now I realized for the first time that it was not rock and roll, TV or movies that had so Americanized my first few years of consciousness in the early 1950s – before all that it was the *Janet and John* readers, the staple fare of so many British infant schools of that time: American productions they were, put out by Harper & Row in New York, where Father wore a snap-brim hat and Mother wore a pencil-slim skirt and high heels while she worked in a fitted kitchen with all mod cons, and Janet and John played on a hedgeless front lawn with a mailbox on a post at the end of the drive. Father flies his own plane, and Janet has racks and racks of new clothes to choose from in every colour under the sun – whoopee! That America – served up to thousands of British kids living in the comparative squalor of immediate post-war Europe, dropping dead from diphtheria and TB, leaving the schoolyard to walk home in the smog past bombsites and prefabs – it must have made a big impression on us before we could even verbalize it. I now knew why these towns with their backdated main streets and peaceful residential roads produced such peculiar and heretofore mysterious emotions in me: they were the images from my first picture books, and they were associated with the cosy, reassuring world of George Eliot Infants School, itself as modern as America, a place of precast concrete and steel rectangles, picture windows, venetian blinds, flush doors, brand-new furniture of tubular steel and moulded plywood, rooms full of sunlight, and beyond them green lawns, silver birch and horse chestnut; and in the afternoon even the odd parental Chevrolet waiting outside the gates to pick up Dean or Cheryl. Many of us toddled home to less ideal surroundings, and for impressionable four-year-old me, at least, Janet-And-John-Town NW8 was a home-from-home, although I didn't see it like that at the time: cultural imperialism had me firmly by the preconscious.

At Dorrance we rejoined I-70, and just a few miles later at Homer we turned off and began looking for a motel along the road to Russell (pop. 5,000). The first one flew the stars and stripes and would probably be expensive, but I checked it out anyway. It was – five bucks above the $25 average. Up at Russell, where a US highway crosses the interstate, there was no end of modern three-storey dormitory blocks to choose from, all of which would offer king- or queen-size beds and a million channels of cable TV; but eventually we found the Monte Carlo – thirty or so white weatherboarded rooms grouped around a rectangular, lawned and tree'd courtyard. It had a refreshingly decaying patina. Our room was old and shabby, but cared for in an un-neurotic kind of way. An arched passage led off to the bathroom. Air-conditioning came through a number of wall vents, rather than a single buzzing and rattling in-room machine – which meant that you could sleep in the cool without earplugs or dreams of trucks. The Josephine Baker story was showing on the public TV channel – Miss Baker returning in triumph to Harlem and declaring she wouldn't appear before segregated audiences. Over on the news, meanwhile, they were rioting in Brooklyn, blacks versus Hasidics; Gorbachev sparred with Yeltsin; Ronald McDahmer stalked the Milwaukee courtroom; and Clarence Thomas, Bush's black nominee to the Supreme Court, was being grilled by a congressional committee. Thomas is a notorious anti-abortionist, and his recent appearance in the limelight seemed to have brought his supporters out on the streets. At this very moment a group of them were picketing a clinic somewhere in Kansas, intent on violently abusing the doctors within, and kicking the shit out of the policemen preventing them. Pro-lifers, they call themselves. Americans don't like to mention the word 'abortion'. Supporters of the process call themselves 'pro-choice'. Just don't mention the operative word at the heart of the issue, folks. Good old American prudery and euphemism in glorious harness. I was reminded of how, back at Duck's Bottom, Ffarington had showed me some drawings of himself in the buff that members of the life class he had modelled for had presented him with: the pictures showed Richard in all his bare glory, except for the area of his crotch, where not a single mark soiled the paper – there was a glaring void where his tackle should have been. One of the artists, perhaps aware of how clumsy an area of virgin white paper looked amidst all the careful shading and highlighting, had opted for the blurred effect that TV uses to disguise the face of certain folks whose identity should not be revealed – alleged criminals, for example. Thus the identity of Richard's genitals was duly protected by a murky erasure. And remembering this event at Duck's Bottom made me recall the number of times we had already heard American women – both live and on TV – engage in a similar coyness by referring to their cunts as their 'front bottom'. No doubt folks will soon be referring to their bums as their 'back front'.

Providence evidently wanted this point about Americans' fear of sex to be underlined that evening in Russell – because after turning the TV off I turned to a 1985 issue of the *National*

Geographic that had been left in the room. There, in a feature about mankind's evolution from hairy ape to *Homo sapiens,* was one of those sequential drawings that showed a series of figures striding from left to right across a double fold-out page. Bringing up the rear, naked and bearded, white and male, as they all were, was *Australopithecus afarensis*; in front of him strode *A. africanus,* then *A. robustus,* and so on through to *Hom. sap. archaic, Hom. sap. neanderthal,* and finally *Hom. sap. modern,* resembling a kind of dreadlocked Steven Spielberg. But I couldn't see how any of these fellows could possibly have evolved from each other. Not that I'm a creationist; it's just that these particular examples of hominid simply were not equipped to reproduce – the most any of them had in the way of sex organs was a vague protoplasmic blob. And this in stark contrast to the loving detail lavished on every other part of their anatomy.

It was par for the course. Nothing had moved since the fifties, when Elvis' hips were forbidden to be shown doing so on TV. And it has not just been a matter of *images* of hips, navels and genitalia. NBC has been known to delete the word 'diaorrhoea' from a chat show, and 'stretch marks' from a sitcom. And in '75 ABC blipped out two words from a Monty Python sketch – the offending phrase being 'naughty bits'. Don't even mention them. And blip 'fuck' from TV movies.

Kansas seemed as everlasting as the national prudery, even though it took us less than a day and a half to get through it. Time passes slowly when you're cruising a near-deserted interstate with few cheerful billboards or bizarre automobiles passing by. Nevertheless it's one of my greatest pleasures to be able to drive for hours on end and feel the gentle monotonous massaging of rubber on road and the slow and steady shifting of scenery. After some days the routine becomes hypnotic, the enormous horizons mesmeric. In western Kansas, where the plains begin to rise steadily, almost imperceptibly, and grain gives way to cattle country, and the land is dotted with eroded outcrops of sandstone, tall bluffs and winding cliffs, and there is no sign of human habitation in any of that prairie (even though the map tells you of one-horse towns on blue highways just over the skyline) – it was along this stretch that we found ourselves being overtaken with dreamlike slowness by a great silver bullet of a motor bus, with high, impenetrably tinted side windows. Once alongside, this monster took a good ten minutes to draw ahead of us – doubtless it was on cruise control – before it finally shifted into our lane. It had no rear windows, and gave only one indication as to who or what it might contain: its tag plate said Tennessee, and the letters read MUSIC. Well now, what country musician was hiding in there? There were hundreds to choose from. We could probably have named twenty at a push. But even if we had been able to name them all a hundred times over we could still have done it before that bus was out of sight. Five, ten, fifteen minutes, a half-hour passed before it was even a half-mile ahead. And after an hour, when it was as far in front as it was possible to see on that dead straight freeway, and it was starting to lose its chromium sheen, we saw it mutate into a small black disc and appear to rise up above the roadway on the shimmering heatwaves, until it was floating there above the horizon like a black hole in the sky, slowly imploding. And at length, with the same steady infinite graduality, it rose further into the air as it shrunk to a pinprick, and at last was finally gone. A strange and most mesmerizing sight to behold. It seemed mysterious, and oddly portentous. Perhaps it had been Elvis himself, having paid a brief visit to earth, taking off again into the realms of space in his silver capsule like some latter-day prophet? Maybe we should write to the *National Enquirer*: 'The windows were dark, but just for a moment Elvis' face appeared at the glass, and he was smiling down on us, and his lips moved, and he was clearly saying "Bless you, good people ... I'll be back ...", and the next thing we knew he was lifted up into the blue heavenly yonder in his great gleaming chariot of light. And, you know, something then told us to turn on our radio, and the strange thing was that every single station just happened to be playing, simultaneously, the King singing 'All My Trials ...' Trouble was, we didn't even have so much as a photograph we could doctor up to fit the facts.

At length we were in Colorado, still climbing through that endless scorched landscape. We stopped at Limon (pop. 1,814), where the main street was one large building site. They were reconstructing after a tornado had recently flattened the place. In a brand-new bar-lounge we ate tacos while the musak machine played the kind of tune that has become staple fare in America:

over a steady, walking-pace rhythm marked out by a domineering, echoing bass drum, accompanied by banks of synthesized violins and vocal chorus, and punctuated every so often by electric guitar solos that soared and wailed in expressions of terrifying anxiety, a male alto poured out his heartache in a cascade of tearful whines. The song's lyric stated no more than the bare fact that his girlfriend didn't want to date him anymore; but how grandiose were its embellishments! Worlds were torn apart by cosmic thunder; grief exploded forth like molten lava from a furious volcano; hopes sky-rocketed into the stratosphere, only to be cataclysmically destroyed and scattered to the four corners of the mournful universe. It was a display of awesome petulance, of a variety that could be found any minute of every hour of every day on 90 per cent of radio stations across the nation.

Now I'm not out to denigrate the kind of emotion one feels when a teenage love affair terminates – it's terribly painful, as everyone knows. But the point is that it is adults who provide most of the market for these tearful outbursts. So how many lonely, misunderstood, tormented, lovelorn hearts aged twenty-one to fifty were out there, still hooked into the bombastic emotional states of their youth? Listening to these cathartic expressions delivered *sans* irony, and *sans* invention save maybe a key modulation for the last chorus? Multitudes.

Adolescent angst expresses itself in a number of ways. The moodiness breaks out into sporadic violence – a punch-up, a broken window, a crashed car, school skipped, and so forth. It's usually containable: life goes on, another lesson learned, thoughts of suicide and revenge pass and another lover is found, and a sexuality is come to terms with. But what happens when lessons are not learned, and when whole generations of lonesome, mixed-up, sexually immature adults are at large, with the freedom to vote, own guns and buy liquor? Turn on the TV news: there's about twenty-five thousand murders a year in the USA, and most of them are about sexual relationships, family or otherwise.

Here, then, could be a good case for *not* preserving one's immediate past: when the landscape of your childhood has changed beyond recognition, then at least you know you can't go back. Perhaps that tornado had done Limon a favour.

*

Soon after leaving Limon to its future, we could see the grey outline of the Rocky Mountains, some eighty miles off. So wide were the horizons all around that a number of isolated thunderstorms could be seen flashing forks to earth all across the plain, and leaving their jagged afterglow. Denver lies in a hollow at the foot of the mountains, and in this sultry early evening light its downtown cluster of highrise towers glowed in glassy, unearthly shades of pinks, greens and blues. Traffic on the urban freeways was thick and fast, heading out in the peak hour rush for the suburbs. North-west towards Boulder the interstate was a blur of speeding Porsches and Mercedes – this was obviously a prosperous neck of the woods, and Boulder itself was a tidy, well-manicured town with a conspicuous dearth of cheap motels. We drove on to Longmont, where the familiar vulgarity of a town strung out for miles along a highway lined with gas stations, fast-fooderies, banks, chiropractors and car showrooms reasserted itself. The first motel we looked at was a prime example of a kind often seen in urban America: its courtyard strung with washing lines and wrecked automobiles and littered with grubby children playing ball, it was a bottom-dollar establishment build of red brick and completely charmless. It was reminiscent of some run-down backstreet in the north of England or some *barrio* in the Third World. This is the kind of place where homeless families find a roof when they first hit town, or itinerant workers stay for the duration. It might make an interesting stop-over. As we waited for the manager to appear a little boy came up and asked me if we had any kids, because the older kids back there playing ball wouldn't let him play with them. He was a skinny little tyke, five years old maybe, with dirty blond hair and crossed blue eyes, and he looked lonely and miserable. God knows what he'd been through on the road with his folks – and it broke my heart to tell him that no, we had no kids and we wouldn't be staying, since there was no sign of anybody to sell us a room and we were too wasted to wait around. He then started to mumble something about a missing teenager that everyone was looking for. I cut away from his pathetic gaze and got back in the car.

Half a mile up the road we checked into the Bar-L, which was aiming for the ranch-style look with its log-timber portico topped by a crudely sculpted miniature white horse. The full-size wooden

stallion standing in the middle of the courtyard looked somewhat surreal, however, since its head was completely overgrown by a bushy growth of creeping vine, bursting with purple flowers.
Inside our room the walls were tongue-and-groove, varnished to a deep brown. Very backwoods. Otherwise it was the reassuring norm: thick brown carpet, enormous double bed, violent-white towels and facecloth, prepacked Ivory brand soap, little coffee-maker with sachets of freeze-dried instant and non-dairy creamer. We used this in the morning, having gone out to fetch a McDonald's breakfast to go with it.

Too much has been said in the way of disparaging criticism against the fast-food chains of the USA for me to have much to add. I have only one real objection to these places – apart from the over-emphasis on beef, which is of course extremely inefficient and wasteful to produce – and this is that you have to stand in line for your food; and, being British, I've done far too much of this already, since table service is a rarity in most ordinary UK establishments. Instead, I offer a modest defence: the thing about McDonalds, and its lesser rival, Hardees, is that, first, the food can be good if you make the right choice: avoid beef, which is often low-quality and overpriced; and avoid the sweets, especially the hot pies, which are mere lumps of microwaved soggy pastry filled with coloured liquid sugar; go for fish, chicken, and salad (which will usually be crisp and fresh). Second, steer clear of these places in cities, where they are usually small and squalid and have no proper tables or chairs; here you also run the risk of being gunned down by an armed maniac. But outside the conurbations a McDonalds or Hardees will often be quiet, pleasantly situated and relaxingly lit. Thirdly, they are not all rigorously uniform, and some offer intriguing local bizarrities, apart from pregnant Amish in Chevy vans. The Hardees on Elvis Presley Boulevard in Memphis, Tennessee has made of itself a shrine to the 'Once and Future King', with a series of paintings around its walls depicting the various stations-in-the-life of Elvis, from early days recording with Sun, through the Pink Cadillac era, GI blues, movie roles, all the way through to the fat-slob-in-a-high-collar years. And elsewhere I've seen mountain folk fresh from church in their Sunday best conduct a long, pious, head-bowed and eyes-closed grace ceremony, with countless call-and-response over the burgers and fries. Served to them, I might add, by the aptly named Miss Widener. But breakfast is what these places are best for, the coffee is often better, and sometimes even newspapers are supplied. At Longmont, we took away a couple of Egg McMuffins, said a quick prayer – always a good idea – ate and checked out.

After this we set off for the mountains. The peculiar thing is that they rise so quickly: just beyond the nearby town of Hygiene the road suddenly bucks and snakes, and in less time than it takes to walk across Hyde Park you're at 10,000 feet and close to the continental divide, surrounded by peaks and pines and picnickers. We admired the scenery, noshed by a lake, and then set off down the mountain again as a wicked storm broke and suddenly things were a little wilder, with torrential rain and vicious hairpins to negotiate with every beat of near-useless wiper blade. With visibility down to an inch we stopped at a roadside shack which was advertising cheap cider, drenched ourselves in the five-yard dash to its door, and were crestfallen to discover that in America not all cider contains alcohol, and not one of the jars in this shop did. So, continuing like the bravest of US postmen ('Neither snow not rain nor heat nor gloom of night stays these couriers from the swift completion of their appointed rounds'), we finally emerged from the mountains at Loveland. And as the clouds slowly cleared and the fifty-mile-an-hour wind began to drop, we made our damp way north on I-25, beginning a 500-mile stint along the eastern margin of the mountains, which would take us well into Montana before we would turn west again on to the Lewis & Clark trail through to northern Idaho. Sixty miles of fast-emptying road brought us to the Wyoming line, quickly past the state capital Cheyenne and thence into Laramie County. In Wyoming, every name you see is the title of some old TV series. And here was mile upon mile of desolate and beautiful rolling prairie. And we thought Kansas had been rather uncrowded. Wyoming is not much bigger in area, but its population is about seven times smaller – that's 400 thousand souls – the population of Edinburgh – spread out across 98 thousand square miles. Makes them hard to spot, even if they have few trees to hide behind.

4. Duck Soup

Rosey and I must have set a record for a couple of tourists in Wyoming: first, we didn't visit Yellowstone National Park; and second, the only horse we saw was the red bucking bronco which adorns the state license plate.

We saw cowboys, though, when we stopped at Chugwater (pop. an optimistic 187). This little town consisted of some fifty yards of anonymous-looking premises on one side of the main street, and on the other side a tall grain silo gilded by the evening sun, which stood alongside the Burlington & Northern railroad tracks. The cowboys in question were sat at a little bar in the general store, a cluttered old place selling everything from cornflakes to pickaxes as well as postcards and Indian-style knicknacks. The men could actually have been country singers, or just ornery dudes really, in denims and Cuban heeled boots, but since this was Wyoming there was at least a chance that they rode the range when they weren't in here quietly chewing the cud with the woman behind the bar. Not long after we'd come in, sat ourselves at a table by the window and been served mugs of coffee, an ordinary-looking fellow walked in, a man in his fifties wearing a short-sleeved plaid shirt and grey shorts. He got himself a toasted ham & swiss and a strawberry malted milkshake, and then cheerfully asked if he might join us.

Initial introductions revealed that he was making his way home from Colorado to Rapid City, South Dakota. And since we knew that Rapid City wasn't too far east of here, close to the Black Hills and the famous national monument of Mount Rushmore, we quizzed him about this extraordinary memorial, where the faces of four renowned presidents – Washington, Jefferson, Lincoln and Teddy Roosevelt – are combined in a gigantic sculpture and gaze forth magisterially from the grey rock of a towering cliff. We were half-inclined to pay it a visit, we said, and our friend duly supplied us with some more information. Then I asked him if he supposed that any latter-day presidents might someday be enshrined alongside the fab four. At this his mood seemed to darken a little.

'I doubt it. I doubt it very much,' he said.

'OK,' I said, 'but just suppose America did decide to carve out another one up there – who would it be? Who would *you* choose?'

About this our friend had no doubt – it would have to be JFK. Fair enough, and fairly predictable. Less predictable was the tack he took from this point on.

'Let me tell you this,' he said, lowering his voice and shooting a nervous glance in the direction of the men at the bar. 'It was the CIA and the Mafia who put away Kennedy, and they've been running this country ever since.'

At this he slapped his newspaper down on the table. 'Do you know what the Recall Act is?' he asked.

He was referring to a recent act of Congress which empowered law enforcement agencies to confiscate property belonging to anyone involved in drug trafficking. The overt purpose of the law had been to discourage smugglers by confiscating their means of transportation – boats, planes, etc. – and even this was, he held, of very dubious legality. But the Recall Act was now gaining notoriety since people convicted of relatively puny crimes such as smoking marijuana in their homes had had their houses and other property taken from them. And our friend – we never discovered his name, but let's call him Frank – was sure that certain people who were irritants to the powers that be were being set up with planted evidence in order that they could be subsequently ruined. He opened the Denver newspaper and pointed out an editorial which complained of one such recent case in that city. Well, said I, at least people were protesting, that was something. Frank was unimpressed: this was the only liberal newspaper left in the West, he said, and they'd soon find a way of shutting it down.

'The Recall Act's in direct violation of the Eighth Amendment that's supposed to protect us against excessive punishment,' he stated. 'It's the worst piece of lawmaking ever enacted in this country.'

And he attacked his sandwich with vehemence.

'What do you do, Frank?'

Frank was a high school teacher. So we asked him about the state of education in the USA. According to him, it was in a sorry state. The infamous recent international comparisons had been correct to put American students bottom of the class. 'Most high school graduates are barely literate,' he said. 'And it's not the fault of their teachers – the few that they have. Education is being shut down. You know what's happening now? They're turning schools into prisons. Literally. In South Dakota they've just closed a couple of schools and made them into penitentiaries.' And he went on: 'I'm a biology teacher. And I've got some students who won't listen to Evolution theory. They don't want me to teach it to them. They say God created it all in seven days, and that's it. They won't hear anything else.'

By now Frank's ham & swiss had thoroughly recharged his road-weary batteries. He began to talk at length about what he saw as the rotten core of the US State. He quickly returned to the nefarious activities of the Government/CIA, between which he saw little difference. From '63 on the CIA had steadily infiltrated the government machinery until now it was completely dominant, with its own man sitting right in the White House. And he related more than one grim story of investigators who had learned too much of the various conspiracies – the Kennedy killing, Iran-Contragate and the rest – and had been pursued and murdered for their pains. As for Clarence Thomas – well, conservatives had been stacking the Supreme Court with their own men since 1963, which gave them a stranglehold on any attempt at redress. 'And you know what they're telling us now? They're saying why make a fuss over Thomas – the Supreme Court is stacked with Bush's men already, one more isn't going to make a difference, so why complain?

'The one really good thing that could come out of what's happening in Russia – and it's what I'm praying for – is that they release the KGB files. The KGB probably knows more about all the crap of the last thirty years than anyone.'

We then heard about the complete destruction of the American economy under Reagan, with figures quoted *en masse* to back all this up. Frank was particularly virulent in his contempt for Reagan's handouts to the rich – he cut their taxes from 70 per cent to 25 per cent, the excuse being (and we'd heard the same thing in

Britain) that this would increase incentives and pump up the economy – and of course the exact opposite had happened. The national debt was gargantuan, industry was folding, banks were crashing, unemployment was sky-rocketing – everything was going down the pan. Frank confessed that he was hoping this 'recession' would turn into a full-scale depression: ' People might just wake up a little to all this shit, then, and make a few changes.' But he wasn't optimistic. 'The more you speak up, the more they sit on you.' He'd been a liberal activist since the sixties, and he'd been audited by the IRS every two years, regular as clockwork. This was pure harassment, in his opinion. The tax authorities only ask for a full exposition of a person's accounts – with all the time, money and effort that this involves – when they suspect that something shady's going on; or else they pick folks at random – so your ordinary citizen might expect to be audited maybe every once in a while. But it looked as if someone had had it in for Frank ever since the days when he protested over Vietnam or led South Dakota's first teachers' strike. It didn't matter that every audit he'd gone through had shown his accounts to be clean – every two years they sat on him.

Our chat with Frank had amounted to a two-hour lecture – diatribe might be more accurate – delivered with extraordinary vigour, and only asking in return the odd head-nod or interrogative prompting on our part. The picture he painted was a sobering one – but there was nothing exceptionally defeatist or pessimistic about the man. His blue eyes never stopped twinkling, and his stocky frame seemed charged with resistance, and relishing of struggle. This didn't appear to be a man discharging a morbid compulsion to unload dreadful fantasies upon strangers. He seemed to have too much of an appetite for life to be one of those. He certainly had an appetite for those baguette-sized toasted sandwiches – he was ordering another one as we parted company.

It was dark when we stepped outside and set off again along the interstate. For a while we were the only people on that road, but before long a pair of headlamps appeared behind us, and sat on our tail for the next fifty miles. CIA? IRS? It wasn't till we were approaching the junction with Highway 20, which led off east to Nebraska and Dakota, that the car finally overtook us, and we saw Frank giving us a wave as he sped off up the slip road. Not long after this we pulled into Douglas, and after avoiding a motel which displayed a large cross on which was written TELEPHONES • HBO • REASONABLE RATES • JESUS IS COMING, we settled for the Vagabond on the other side of Main Street, stocked up from its ice machine, and drunk bourbon in front of CNN's garish fare. Next morning when we breakfasted at Fat Ed's diner, the Spanish-Indian waitress insisted we leave her with our autographs, since we were the first live English she'd ever met. We also left her with a 10p piece; she loved the Queen's head.

Beyond Caspar, I-25 descends for fifty miles to the Powder River and then climbs up again to Buffalo, where the bank gave us lollipops and coffee while they processed our credit cards; and in the town's quaint old Rexall drugstore (complete with little bar and soda fountain) Rosey bought Larry Gonick's *Cartoon History of the Universe*, whose multi-billion year timespan helped put the tribulations of America's past thirty years into some sort of perspective. Out of Buffalo, I-25 turned into I-90 for another long and gradual descent through that beautiful and desolate country towards Montana and the Bighorn Valley. Here the road follows the little Bighorn River through miles of scruffy-looking lowland dotted with clumps of poplars, along highway that hasn't yet been improved to interstate standard, and through communities which were strictly rough-and-ready: beat-up trucks, shabby farmsteads, no sign of commercial development or any other kind of investment. It was inexpensive.

This isn't too surprising when you consider that the land hereabouts is the site of one of white America's most spectacular humiliations: General Custer's defeat at the hands of the Sioux in the summer of 1876. It's as if the whites have been happy to steer clear of it ever since that time. Not that it has been left to the Sioux, of course, who were massacred not long after at Wounded Knee. The 'Custer Battlefield' and the other three thousand or so square miles are now a Crow Indian reservation. Back in the 1870s the Crow and the Sioux were disputing ownership of this land, and many Crow imagined that by siding with the white man they would aid their cause. Which is the reason why some of them scouted for Custer, and others gave these scouts cute names such as White-Man-Runs-Him.

We learned a little of this particular chunk of history at the

Bighorn County Historical Museum & Visitors' Center at Hardin, where a relative of one of those Crow scouts was on hand to chat to us – a handsome, soft-voiced tall fellow in blue denims and meat hat who picked out a postcard, upon which was a sepia photograph of a young man with long plaited hair wearing an ordinary white man's work shirt. This man's name appeared less derogatory than White-Man-Runs-Him, or Two-Faced-Uncle-Tom, or whatever – he went by the name of Curly, and our native American guide claimed to be his sister's great-grandson. And yes, we could see a likeness, especially with the shirt.

Interstate 90 now hooked west and drew us into Billings late that evening. Billingsgate would be more appropriate. It stank: oil refinery, sewage works, power stations, sulphurous stacks – we drove through the lot on the way out to the smaller town of Laurel, where we found the better class of accommodation; here at the Russell Motel we were given what amounted to a large apartment for next to nothing. Leaving Laurel the next morning, hitting open country again at the Stillwater County line, we saw another set of Coffindaffer crosses, resplendent at the edge of a hayfield. So he'd made it this far. At least none of the crosses I had seen had been burning yet, or had anyone nailed up on them. It has always been a source of wonder to me that Christians, who are often in the vanguard of protests against the spread of violent and sexual imagery – images purported to be encouraged by non-religious 'liberals' – have never had any scruples about disseminating their own famous icon of a near-naked man being tortured to death on a cross. Lenny Bruce once made a similar point when he imagined that the Jewish equivalent of this behaviour might be to wear little model gas chambers around their necks.

We did a long day's drive out of Laurel – 350 miles through Montana's big skies, through the Bozeman Pass, and then across the continental divide near Butte, from where it was all downhill to Missoula. As may already be evident, describing American mountains is not my strong suit. It's not that driving through them on an interstate is unenlightening in the sense that the views are not 100 per cent spectacular and awesome – they are. The downhill stretch from Butte, which follows and constantly criss-crosses the twists and turns of the Clark Fork River, is a series of tremendous peaks, huge gorges and enormous valleys that are a

wonder to behold and make the Appalachians look like Hampstead
Heath. It's just that, essentially, there's nothing going on; or as the
bumper stickers have it – shit happens. Now this state of nothing-
happensness can be, as any Buddhist knows, a state of ultimate
enlightenment, which is fine except that it's not communicable in
words. There is a famous painting, though, which comes very
close to describing a rapid drive through the northern Rockies. It is
Le Château des Pyrénées, by René Magritte, and it depicts a very
large grey rock suspended in air. On top of this rock is a stone
castle (not a Villa) and the whole ponderous mass hovers above an
ocean. So, take the castle away, and attach in its place a steering
wheel, and imagine you are sitting on this rock holding the wheel;
that's what it feels like.

Missoula, which sits in a wide valley at 3,000 feet, is something
of a ski resort in winter. In late August its main slope is a bare,
dirty brown hill with a giant white M cut into it, below which sits a
town of thirty thousand folks, with a lot of motels, liquor stores
and restaurants. Rather than try the Italian, Greek or Mexican, we
preferred to sample the vernacular 'family' restaurant, staple fare
of American towns, and usually good for unpretentious and cheap
(inexpensive) food, if you don't mind going without beer or wine,
because of course 'families' don't drink beer or wine. You also
have to do it all before 10 p.m., which is when they close up. Our
waitress at the family restaurant in Missoula was the spitting
image of – damn – what was the name of that actress who starred
with Fred MacMurray in *Double Indemnity*? I couldn't recall the
name, even though I saw plenty of her face, since she was one of
those many American waitresses loath to leave you alone for two
minutes without coming up to enquire cheerfully if everything's
OK. My burger and fries was fine except that it tasted of cinnamon
– but this came as no surprise, since Americans put cinnamon in
everything they cook. Rosey's salad dressing, picked from the
usual choice of 'FrenchItalianBlueCheeseThousandIslandor-
Ranch?' was almost pure sugar, and both looked and tasted like
grenadine. This too was par for the course. America has a very
sweet tooth. It's surprising it has any teeth left. It certainly makes
for a lot of fat people. I had been entertaining the notion that out
West I'd see fewer examples of blubbery corpulence, but to my
surprise the more time zones we crossed the more I saw, which

was startling because I'd always imagined that folk would somehow be more active out here. Perhaps the sight of a series of presidents and public figures collapsing on the jog – including the man credited with the 'invention' of jogging, who died in his sneakers – has since driven folk back to their cars and couches and comfort food. And their beer, of course. American beer is that stuff wherein all the alcohol has been turned to sugar. (America rigorously states the alcohol content of all bottles of wine or spirit, but it is never to be found printed on any beer can. No room for all the decimal points, I guess.) So after our meal of sugar and cinnamon, and three-quarters of an hour spent racking my brains for the name of that actress, we left. On the way out, triumphant at last, I told the girl she looked like Barbara Stanwyck. She'd never heard of her.

Our room at the Canyon Motel had a Harley-Davidson parked to the right of it and a black VW hippy bus from North Carolina parked to the left. More importantly, it had cable TV, and what's more this included C-Span, a channel devoid of commercial interruptions which is dedicated to the coverage of political events, in Congress and elsewhere. I'd already praised this instrument of democracy whilst witnessing chunks of the Thomas hearings. Tonight C-Span was covering an interesting one – the Libertarian Party's presidential candidates' debate. The *what* party?

The view one had of these proceedings was based on a single camera shot which never varied: it was a view of a simple podium, flanked on each side by a table and chair. The backdrop appeared to be the wall of a marquee. Conducting affairs was a nervous-looking lank-haired woman in her thirties. The two candidates sat at their respective tables beside the podium: one was a middle-aged white man with a full beard who smiled a lot without using his eyes; the other was a younger black man who wore round steel-rimmed glasses and never smiled once. I can't tell you what the audience was like because there was never a view of them – but they were pretty quiet. But the three protagonists at the platform had one thing in common, and that was an air of intense discomfort. Intriguing; not what one usually associates with American political parties, or at least the only two that I had ever been aware of up till now. So – what were these people about?

The speeches that followed from each candidate soon made it

clear. They wanted what might best be described as right-wing
anarchy: no taxes *whatsoever*; no gun laws; no restrictions on an
individual's right to do whatever he or she wants, anytime,
anyplace. After the two speeches the lank-haired woman read out
questions apparently culled from the audience in advance. There
was no debate as such – no actual locking of horns between the
two contenders – perhaps they didn't want to tarnish their party's
image with any show of conflict; and there was practically no
disagreement between the two as they responded to the questions
in turn. Both were firmly resolved that, were they to become
Presnightstates, they would not be flying around in Airforce One
and wasting the taxes which of course would be non-existent by
then. Just how they intended to finance even the barest of national
structures without taxes was never made clear; perhaps they
thought they could do it all by playing the stock markets, or maybe
they would take a leaf out of the medieval book and make like
Queen Elizabeth with seasonal progresses around the country,
landing on people's doorsteps and gently extorting bed, breakfast
and all the cash in the mattress. The only ripple of controversy
came when the shifty-looking young lawyer had to deal with the
question of abortion. Yes indeed, said this Sidney Poitier
lookalike, he was pro-choice, and therefore pro-party line on the
issue; however, he confessed that in his 'private and personal'
belief, life began at conception. Whatever this implied, he wasn't
saying, and he wasn't pressed on the point either, since Libertarian
Party procedure did not allow cross-examination or follow-up
questions. The other issue where the Libertarian Party comes
close to left-wing liberals is over drugs – they want to legalize
them all, contending that 'It's up to the individual what he or she
wants to put into his body', and so on. Although I'm sure they
would have no program for addicts, and no wish for any State
controls.

So – a bunch of fruitcakes, perhaps, and pretty harmless? A
number of things were disquieting about these people. Firstly,
although some members may have relished their newly won TV
coverage as a chance to get their message across to the nation at
large, I couldn't help suspecting that they may have been happier
sidling up to people in bars where, out of the public eye, they
could put their real program across. What would this be? All I can

say is that on C-Span they were coming over like Nazis trying to be respectable for the camera; a bunch of embarrassed brownshirts whose tent-show had been interrupted by an enquiring lens. Secondly, they had won the right to TV coverage on account of the fact that they now had a Congressman in Washington – the candidate with the beard, the member for Alaska, no less. Thirdly, this man bore a most uncomfortable resemblance to the South African fascist Eugene Terreblanche. What they were promoting was the all too familiar weak-to-the-wall-and-the-rich-round-the-pool stuff that was only a grenade-toss away from Bush–Reagan Republicanism. I began to wonder about our friend Frank's hopes that the recession slide even deeper. He may have been forgetting about the kind of slime that tends to ooze out of the woodwork in times like these.

There was more interesting TV to behold next morning, which was Saturday. Children's TV it was, on ABC. After Sylvester and Tweetie Pie came *Rosey*, a cartoon starring a child gangleader drawn to look like Roseanne Arnold and bearing the unmistakable voice of Arnold herself. So, not content with her prime-time sitcom, Roseanne was now going after the kids. I thought this episode was rather telling: Rosey and her gang had to liberate the treehouse from a couple of bespectacled, eggheaded boys who used long words and had installed a telescope up there – intelligent kids, in other words. Ah, but how arrogant they were! And sure enough, Rosey's basic butch trickery won out in the end; hard not to conclude that there was a simple message here: it's anti-American to use words of more than one syllable, and to have an interest in astronomy. Galileo would have related to this problem. And *Rosey* reminded me of that British hero of the fifties who regularly appeared on the cover of *Eagle* comic: Dan Dare, 'Pilot of the Future', a muscular, jut-jawed fellow whose arch enemy was the Mekon (Me con? Mekong? Comecon?), another creature with an exceedingly large brain, but whose vast intelligence somehow never managed to prevail over his low-brow opponents. And I thought humankind had got where it is today because of large brains and sophisticated use of language; at least that's what evolutionists say, and that's what Larry Gonick tells us in his *Cartoon History of the Universe* – but then again, evolutionists are suspect in America today as the Neanderthal species makes its comeback bid; and as for Mr Gonick, he's got a large bald head and he wears spectacles – and you can never trust a word these Cro-Magnons tell you. *Superman* is, of course, the *reductio ad absurdum* of the Neanderthal fantasy, for the 'Man of Steel' never prevails through any great powers of analysis, but only via brute force and a number of implausible motor and sensory attributes. America can thank its lucky stars that none of these Rosey/ Superman brutes had much of a hand in drafting its constitution.

The other notable aspect of that morning's TV was the commercials. Mostly they were what you would expect: ads for breakfast cereals, Just-Say-No-To-Drugs spots, and so on; but right in the middle of all this wholesome stuff there suddenly exploded graphic scenes of guns blasting off, sliced-up corpses, cop cars and fist fights, as a late-night cops-and-violence show was trailed. And then it was back to fluffy bunnies and the rest. This was a perfect example of the kind of incongruity I was well used to by now: this dipolar America, this constant fluctuation between ruthlessness and sentimentality. It is something this country has been well noted for, and examples are legion: the stubble-faced, tough commie-hunter Nixon rolls out his 'Checkers' speech, invoking the image of a poor little puppy; the 'sixties' – a strange combination of serious revolutions and simple-minded flower worship; William Dean Howells' famous statement that 'What America wants is a tragedy with a happy ending' – does this explain the enormous attraction for them of the Christian myth of Christ crucified and resurrected?; butch footballers clash in heavy armour while their fluffy cheerleaders wave tinsel from the sidelines; a movie industry which turns out gratuitous violence alongside Walt Disney and *Terms of Endearment*; firearms in every home, and sugar on every table; the very landscape, vast emptiness or cluttered commerciality; the weather – relentlessly hot or relentlessly cold, but no middle ground; the notices outside Baptist churches: 'Heaven or Hell – Your Choice' – no grey areas; the goods, overpriced or underpriced, no middle ground; 'America – Love it or Leave it' – it's a simple choice, buster. It's often been said that it takes a Britisher – someone from a land of shifting mists and unsettled weather – to experience the American either/or syndrome as extraordinary; to see something odd in the way a nation flag-waves its fighting sons off to war and then ties yellow ribbons round the oak trees. However, it's a British poet who comes most strongly to mind when considering all this; for isn't it all very Blakeian: from blood running down palace walls to 'Little lamb, who made thee?'? From Blake's fearsome myths of violent gods to his mawkish songs of innocence, there's not much middle ground here. Is that why they called him Mad Blake? Is there something a touch psychopathic about these extremes of mood? Perhaps. But I read America as I read Blake: one moment I'm exhilarated by the enormous strength and audacity of its courage and invention; the next I'm thinking 'This is extremely soppy.' And the image of Wet America that haunted me most on this trip was of a duck. Not Donald Duck, who is a mean, miserly sonofabitch; not Daffy Duck, who is at least sometimes amusing; not Howard the duck, who was a conspicuous failure; but an anonymous duck, a generic duck – a duck seen in every gift shop, coffee shop, home and motel. Sometimes in three dimensions, a china figure or a woodcarving, but usually in two, adorning place-mats, calendars, crockery, tablecloths, bed linen, bumper stickers. It is found on lawns, windowsills, kitchen shelves. It is a standing duck, seen in profile, looking straight ahead. And it has a ribbon round its neck, tied in a bow. This universal, beribboned duck has no name, and no history that I have been able to discover. But by the time we reached Missoula (where a china one stood in that restaurant's window), this symbol of domestic America was getting a little irritating. And matching this annoyance at the unbearably cute, as we left town that midday, there now came a sense of mild foreboding: ever since our conversation with Frank at Chugwater a kind of darkness had touched the incidents along our route: the sobering experience of the Custer Battlefield; the smell of Billings, and the sight of Coffindaffer dogging our tracks; and the sound of those gruesome-looking Libertarians morosely parading their wares. And this was added to by the knowledge that along today's route up to Sandpoint, Idaho, was a notorious little community of Nazis, complete with their own church (the Church of Jesus Christ Christian-Aryan Nations), who had recently been happily murdering and bombing anyone who spoke out against them. We ourselves weren't planning on visiting their community at Hayden Lake, but it all helped add up to a strange feeling as we

rolled down the mountain toward Coeur d'Alene: it was all
sweetness and dark.

We were soon through Lookout Pass in the Bitteroot Mountains,
over the Idaho line, and down into Coeur d'Alene, which lies at
the southern end of the Idaho panhandle, some 100 miles south of
the Canadian border. This is a relatively low-lying area, thick with
pine forest and lakes, but one is seldom out of sight of the high
peaks of the Bitteroots away to the east. Coeur d'Alene means
'Spikeheart' – the early trappers' name for the local Indians, who
apparently drove upsettingly hard bargains. Here we put four
thousand miles of interstate driving behind us for the time being
and took off north on Highway 95, a busy two-lane road through
thick conifer forest which didn't allow for many views apart from
Canadian license plates, which jostled for space amongst Idaho's
own 'Famous Potatoes' tag, a slogan that more than a few
Idahoans find extremely unflattering.

Forty miles on we crossed the northern arm of Lake Pend
Oreille and entered Sandpoint, a compact little town, still pretty
much undeveloped, with just its little grid of nineteenth-century
buildings plus the odd glass-fronted bank or two. Hereabouts was
where we aimed to be spending the next couple of weeks, courtesy
of the Fourniers, Rosey's acquaintances of years back, whom she
had met whilst working at that same Swiss resort where she'd
known Ed and Jenny Bauer. And apparently we'd have our own
condominium to stay in, close to the lake. We drove out of town a
few miles before turning on to a rough lakeside road, along which
we searched for the home of our hosts. We had the number, but
we spotted it by virtue of its mailbox, which was painted pale blue
and adorned with coloured flowers – clearly the work of Katie
Fournier. We knew little about Clark and Katie Fournier, except
that Katie was a painter who sent Rosey wonderfully ornate
Christmas cards, and Clark was supposed to be a writer who
worked as a ski instructor in the winter, down in the south of the
state at the Sun Valley resort. Having had repeated invitations over
the years to visit their lakeside home, this year and this trip had
seemed ideal for taking up the offer; and driving along the serene
shoreline of Lake Pend Oreille, we were looking forward to a
week or two off the road in surroundings such as these.

Opposite Katie's decorated mailbox we turned on to a little winding dirt track, and immediately stopped to admire the view: on either side of us was a hayfield, smattered with blue and yellow flowers and rippling in the breeze. A couple of hundred yards ahead we could see a large house of blue-grey timber, half-hidden by stands of tall cottonwoods which angled upwards in a gentle arch. Immediately to the right was a rough patch of woodland, and beyond this the hayfield stretched down to the lakeside, which glimmered in the hot sun; beyond, triangles of great green mountain towered over the distant shore. It would have made any nineteenth-century French landscape painter squirm with delight, from Corot to Cézanne. The Nez Percé Indians probably charged those trappers for the view alone: 'You want paint this – you give us many beads and fire-sticks.'

'*Merde* on these spikehearts,' thinks Jean-Luc before coughing up and setting down his easel.

We rolled on in under the trees and drew up by the house next to a couple of gleaming new sedans, at the edge of a lawn which led down to the water's edge. Beyond were the wide expanses of Lake Pend Oreille and the mountains rising from the far shore like an image from a Chinese hexagram: the still mountain above the joyous lake. As we climbed out from the Datsun's sweat-pit a slim young woman in a skimpy bathing suit emerged from the house and skipped across to greet us.

Katie was like some kind of nordic bendy toy. She had long honeyblonde hair and bright blue eyes deep-set above prominent cheekbones. She made a tidy contrast to the beefy Clark, who moments later emerged dripping from the lake and strode towards us in a pair of tiny red bollock-huggers. Short and heavily tanned, he sported thick black hair, sideburns and a substantial moustache. In fact he was the spitting image of Gabriel Garcia Marquez – although, unlike Ed Bauer, who was always being stopped and asked for Boris Becker's thumbprint, Clark said no Marquez fans ever harassed him.

We went inside and cracked some beers. The Fournier's house, which Clark had designed and built from local timber, was basically one vast high-ceilinged living room with everything else leading off it, including a deck outside which looked over the lake. It oozed wealth and comfort: deep pile carpets, cumulo-nimbus sofas, caged parrots, heavy tinted-glass dining table, big stone fireplace, heavyweight beams and rafters ... a real ski instructor's fantasy. Clark had by now donned a towel bathrobe and spread himself across a sofa. He spoke with a heavy drawl, and tended to roll his eyes upwards until the pupils disappeared, which gave the impression that he was constantly about to pass out. Meanwhile Katie sat with her knees drawn up and her eyes shining and introduced us to their two kids – the three-year-old Carrie, dark and plump and prone to striking very adult-looking poses; and the five-year-old Tom, who looked like Jack Nicholson and appeared to be a quiet and thoughtful chap. He was coming up to school age now, but his parents expressed serious doubts about the competence of the school system and said they would prefer to tutor him at home; however, this coming week they were starting the school year by 'trying him out' at a local kindergarten to see how he went and if he liked it there. They might send him along 'a couple of days a week' – 'But really,' said Clark, indicating the child's immediate environment with a wave of his hand, 'it's all here, isn't it? Nature ... everything. This is where you learn. We can teach him all he needs to know right here.'

Neither would the kids be corrupted by radio, newspapers or TV, because Clark and Katie did not subscribe. Another TV-free household? Almost. It turned out they watched tapes – movies for the parents and the ubiquitous *Sesame Street Christmas Show* for the kids. But Clark was particularly keen to emphasize his anti-establishment stance. We were telling him of our (not unpleasant) encounters with the cops in Fruitland and Brazil, and this drew a vigorous response: 'I hate cops,' he said. 'I hate all authority. All they do is fucking waste your time ...' and he went on to tell us how he'd recently been done for speeding; pulled over by a lawman, Clark had asked what the trouble was and been told that he'd been clocked at ninety-plus. Recounting, Clark reproduced the explosive indignation he had clearly felt at the time: 'I let that cop have it, man, I always do, I *never* take shit from a cop – "You can't do this," I told him, "you're just running a speed trap here, that's all this is, a *speed trap,* man!"' And he rolled his eyes.

We waited for the story to continue, but apparently that was it. As far as Clark was concerned, speed traps were a violation of his civil rights. He then told us how they were being constantly harassed by police and federal helicopters flying low to inspect their land for signs of cannabis cultivation. Again, this routine example of law-enforcement seemed to upset Clark to an exaggerated degree. For all his comforts, he was exhibiting signs of a siege mentality.

Katie was less troubled. She showed us where we'd be staying – not, as previously supposed, at a relative's apartment in town, but right here, in a camper trailer parked under the trees at the edge of the woods. We were impressed: we'd be waking up to all this lake, mountain, wood, wildflower and fresh air. We exclaimed that it really was a terrible, awful place. It took Katie a moment or two to latch on to the sarcasm.

We got ourselves organized in the camper and went to bed early, and we luxuriated in a lie-in till the following afternoon. We finally emerged to a blustery day and a brisk wind chopping up the lake, upon which a small twin-berth sailboat was anchored nearby. This turned out to belong to friends of the Fourniers, Bob and Darlene Springer. Bob was tall and quiet and amiable, a chubby fellow with a mass of grey curls and a heavy moustache. His wife Darlene appeared contrastingly careworn, a little overweight and baggy-eyed. They had two kids, a heavily built fourteen-year-old called Selma, and a ten-year-old blond boy with large spectacles called Milt. While the women and children sat around indoors, Clark and Bob and we two visitors drank wine by the waterside and took turns to go out on runs in Clark's Bobcat catamaran, an excellent little toy. Clark and Bob had a well-practised double act: Bob the straight man, Clark wild and talkative, as they cracked a stream of more-or-less private jokes and generally buffooned about. Clark called Bob 'Captain'; Bob called Clark 'Commander'. It transpired that Cap'n Bob's boat had been recently acquired and he wasn't an experienced sailor, whereas Commander Clark was well-used to the waves and had spent some time in the past chartering out boats in the Caribbean, and was now tutoring his buddy in seamanship in preparation for a holiday in the West Indies that the two families were planning to take together soon.

At sundown the Springers departed in their boat, and later that evening when the kids were abed we four dined around that smoked-glass table. Clark, a little reticent, told us something of his

childhood back east, and of a fairly unhappy time with a
domineering father. And there was a large oil painting of Katie's
which hung on the wall above us. It was something of an
exception to the rest of her work, which was well represented
around the house and tended to joyful and elaborate watercolour
and felt-tip renditions of unicorns and fairies and leaping horses
with flowing manes. But this picture was conspicuously different,
apart from being the only oil painting on view. It looked to be
based on an early, pre-cubist Picasso, of a young man posing with
a horse, and used the same red-dominated pallette. However, in
this case the young man was now a young woman and, unlike the
original figure, she was looking directly at the viewer. It was a
self-portrait, Katie holding the reins of this white horse, and
looking most serious and disquieted. I was impressed by the
technique, and more so when I learned that Katie was self-taught.
But when I asked her about the picture she was either unable or
unwilling to discuss it other than to say that she was unaware of
the Picasso that it seemed to echo.

Clark had no qualms about publicizing his own intentions – he
wanted to break into Hollywood, and when he wasn't busy with
real estate deals he was writing movie scripts to that end. And
once he had ascertained that script-reading was something I did he
was keen to have me read his work. So I gladly took his typescript
back to the trailer that night.

Many readers will tell you that after some time in the job a
certain sixth sense comes into play which enables one to judge a
script without even taking it from the envelope. I wouldn't go this
far; it's never worked with me except when the address was
written in crayon; but once debagged there are plenty of telling
signs to watch for. First, the binding. If it isn't bound at all, one is
none the wiser – the best and the worst come like this. Likewise if
it's in stiff covers from a professional printing and binding service
it could be magnificent or it could be a howling dog. But beware
illustrations – these mean one is going to have to earn one's fee the
hard way. There seems to be no logic behind this, and it has
nothing to do with the quality of the picture(s). Nevertheless, an
illustration is the kiss of death. Likewise if the script has been
penetrated with a hole punch and then either been placed in a ring-
binder or had green string threaded through the holes and tied in a

bow – then again you're in for a tiresome read. Next, the typeface.
Top copies of scripts from manual typewriters are getting rarer but
they still turn up, and this evidence of absent-mindedness is
always mysteriously coupled to a lack of talent. And such
offerings which also come with stage directions in red have
produced some of the most mind-numbing works in the history of
the written word. However, the kind of machine used is no clue at
all: the worst work can come off an Apple Mac and the best from
a '26 Remington. Nevertheless, a vivid mixture of bolds, romans
and italics and every other optional extra usually indicates an
author more in love with the Amstrad than the work at hand and
who has thereby successfully divorced medium from message.
Next comes the title. Often gives little away, unless it contains the
first name of somebody famous, e.g. Vladimir Illych, Adolf,
Marilyn or Wolfgang. Last names by themselves also guarantee
tedium, viz. *Trotsky, Byron, Savanorola, Monroe* or *Mozart*. The
worst script I have ever entertained came in an enormous ring-
binder complete with illustrations, a very long introduction
(another danger sign – and this one was longer than the script
itself), was a top copy in black, red, bold and italic, and was called
Socrates. Pass the hemlock.

Taking out Clark's script I saw it had none of those no-no's. I
started in on the familiar American IBM typeface and 8½ x 11
format. That's the trouble with American scripts – they are always
so uniformly professional, they don't give you a clue.

The title was ordinary enough, but not quite forgettable: I do
remember that it contained the word 'island'. The story concerned
boat-chartering and gun-running in the Caribbean. It was a buddy
movie dealing with two easy-going guys who get involved with an
evil, firearm-smuggling oriental and carry out all sorts of carry-ons
upon the ocean whilst their respective wives fret about on shore
wondering what has happened to their men. What surprised me
was that despite all the drugs and danger and lovingly
choreographed fist fights, nobody got killed or even badly hurt. No
tragedy at all, though happy ending it did have – the boys come
home and trudge exhaustedly up the jetty and into the arms of their
overjoyed, 'attractive' wives.

It was a don't-give-up-your-day-job number. In fact it was a
have-you-considered-extending-your-day-job-to-nights-and-

weekends? number. I was disappointed. I'd read plenty of crap movie scripts but I'd never before been the guest of the author. I tried to keep things in proportion: for every bad aspiring Hollywood script there's a worse one that Hollywood uses, I told myself. But I couldn't tell Clark that. I could tell him there was nothing wrong with the scenario, inasmuch as 'Sub-Hemingwayesque Adventure in the Caribbean' could be called a scenario. And Hollywood liked titles with words like 'beach', 'park', 'cape', and 'island', didn't they? We could rework it to something like *Cape Island, Park Beach* or *Beach Park*. I went to sleep with visions of Clark and Bob charging about the Caribbean drinking rum and smoking reefer and outwitting evil Japanese men while Katie and Darlene bit their nails and looked anxiously out to sea from the kitchen window.

In the morning I had a swim in the warm waters of the lake, and afterwards I sat on our hosts' little sandy beach soaking up the sun and telling Clark what I thought of his script. Yeah – this was where you discussed big movie projects in the USA: beneath a parasol, sun glinting on the water, glasses clinking, blonde in the background, yachts in the distance. I plied him with Myers while trying desperately to curb my gift for encouraging people – but in vain. He took my criticisms happily on board and talked enthusiastically of rewrites. But he was outspokenly *not* interested in the politics of the area his story was set in. Surprising, if only because so much useful violence and adventure comes from that source. Anyway, we had a lot of fun playing with those titles.

Clark said he was an admirer of Melville's *Billy Budd* and he lent me his copy. Later on I bunked up with it in the back of the camper under canvas and mosquito net, to the sound of the distant lapping waves. Budd is this gorgeous, tragic sailor – imagine Brando, Brad Davies, Willem Dafoe or Jack Kerouac in the part – an innocent seaman falsely accused of mutiny by a master-at-arms who, suffering from sexual guilt, is attempting to get rid of the object of his desire, i.e. Billy. The upshot is that Billy Budd finally swings from the yard arm. Or you could say he was crushed to death by a very heavy closet. I was impressed. But what had attracted Clark to this tragedy-with-an-unhappy-ending? Maybe he related to the master-at-arms' problem, or maybe like Billy he felt persecuted? Whatever it was, Clark wasn't very forthcoming –

'Just a great story' – but he did confess that he hadn't seen the homoerotic angle at all. Curious.

And there was another curious thing about Clark. It slipped out that he had once 'started a church' in the neighbourhood. We were very interested in this, but it was clear that Clark was unhappy his wife had mentioned it, and we learned no more about the mysterious church and what it may or may not have been (and still might be?) promoting, save that tax avoidance came into it.

After that Labor Day Monday Clark was off to work and the boy Tom was off to kindergarten and things quietened down for the week. We saw little of Clark over the next few days, but had many an amiable chat with Katie when she wasn't busy in her studio at the back of the house. The two kids hung around the camper a lot. Tom never stopped asking questions – about how the gas stove worked, about books, about the history of the universe, about the food we cooked, about anything he saw us doing and everything that caught his eye. He was hungry. I couldn't help but wonder what he might already be missing out on – like the wonderful world of the media, which wouldn't be nearly so instructive if it were any less grotesque. He spent only two days that week in kindergarten. His little sister made quite a contrast. Carrie seemed far more concerned with her image than with the workings of the world. And she had an unnatural amount of tension in her little shoulders, which were hunched into a permanent shrug as she switched from one studied pose to another. Her favourite stance was to stand with her legs crossed and hold an elbow in one hand while the other supported her tilted face, and her lips pouted and her big eyes beamed in on you. While her brother sought facts, Carrie sought attention and pretended to be at an endless cocktail party.

We sought out Sandpoint and explored the place. My first impression of it, and the north-west in general, was of less overt consumerism and a good deal fewer churches in evidence than back east, where the houses of God and their kerbside signboards had crammed the highway: REVIVAL, ALL WELCOME; TRUMPETING NOBLE TRUTH MINISTRIES; YE MUST BE BORN AGAIN; HOLY GHOST PREACHING – HEAVEN BLUE, HELL HOT ... whilst up here it was a change not to be constantly screamed at by folks touting everything from Jesus Christ to J.C. Penney. However, on one side of Sandpoint's railroad tracks, away from the downtown shops and banks and rough-timbered tourist mall, we found an area of schools and residential blocks populated with an alarming number of churches of all sorts of denomination – churches of God, churches of Christ, churches of Religion and so forth, all modestly announcing themselves. But we didn't find any with the word 'Aryan' or 'Clark Fournier' in the title.

There was a time when I beheld churches with utmost terror and trepidation. I was very young – four or five years old – and would sometimes wander into a local temple. I thrilled to the Catholic buildings in particular – the thorny, bloody horror of Christ, the zomboid expressions of saints and martyrs; but every Christian church was a shadowy place, saturated with morbid preoccupations and reeking of decay. They were to me strange, dark tumours lurking within the body of the community; houses of fear, where people did incomprehensible things, the most baffling of which was this constant admission of sin and guilt. I could not relate to this at all: it did not apply to me, it was a nonsense. Later on I was to read about show trials in Germany and under Stalin and I could see the same mechanism at work: innocent people brainwashed by repetition and ritual until they were convinced of their own personal wickedness, and subsequently took slavish delight in confessing this loudly. A simple, universal and efficacious means of social control. My fear of churches abated early on, but the fascination has remained.

I went to church in the USA. It was in 1988 and I'm still trying to wash the tack off. It was in one of Pickens County's many beauty spots – Pleasant Valley or Sleepy Glade or Nice View or Cute Hollow or Mellow Grove or Hobbiton-over-the-Water – such places abound in the Piedmont district. This one was the Neat Lawns Baptist Church, Pastor Duane Nuremberg, a local electrician.

In the South, churches come in two genres: rich and poor; and as a general rule they divide along lines of race. The black churches have the more humble buildings – old stores, ex-private houses, breezeblock huts; the whites have invested in purpose-built structures, and grander materials. But the ideal model is universal: a simple Greek temple with a spire on top. From the outside, Neat Lawns displays no sign of the cross; it could be some local government building, except perhaps for the little spire – not rising forth from any tower, not organic, but merely a quote – very postmodern; a Greek temple married to a gothic spike. A marriage made in blood: Hellenistic orgies of hot revenge and stoic angst, plus the muddy frost of northern winters, in this conjunction of quote upon quote, roof upon roof, the steep pitch of central Europe seated upon the flat-angled Mediterranean pediment. A classical temple with a pointy hat, a reminder of inquisitions and of Goya's manacled and conical-capped prisoners. A contemporary evocation of the Age of Enlightenment in red brick, grey slate, white timber and coloured glass. The spire perches top-heavy over the portal like Luther astride a bucking Aeschylus; this is the house of Clytemnestra and Agamemnon, Solon, Socrates, Xenon, Dracon, Cassandra, their retinues, their slaves. And supporting the pediment, four slim white pillars stand in for the horses of the Apocalypse: Conquest, War, Judgement, Death & Hell & Famine. The plain design of this portico suggests the Doric order, which in turn implies a military edge to things; the building could almost be a barrack hall. But this is grandiose by the South's standards. There's many a southern church which presents the frontage of an ordinary private house to which has been added just a noticeboard, and incongruously atop the roof a little dunce's cap of papier mâché or plywood.

Inside, Neat Lawns is plain as a school assembly hall, bare walls, simple wooden pews. Apart from the fitted carpet, that is, and up front a solid collection of classical panelling, the finely worked lecterns, pulpit and choir stalls. It's Easter Sunday and a good-sized, well-dressed and adequately fed congregation is filing in. Not normally one to lower the tone of a church service with my presence, my curiosity has today won out, and I have dragged Larry Keith and Ffarington along with me. Larry introduces me to the pastor, who smiles at me, and I can see fear and suspicion in his hard eyes. Presently he stands on the podium in his grey suit and steel-rimmed spectacles and welcomes us all: there's a hundred people here today, and it's a record (I ruefully reflect that I'm to blame for this), so let's get started with the parade of mothers and babies. And so we do. To the strains of a Hammond Organ, a file of mothers-and-babies emerges from a side door and shuffles very shyly around in front of the podium and then off through another side door. It takes about a minute. Then Pastor Nuremberg calls them back. They were supposed to walk right around the congregation, 'and give everyone a good look'. So the parade re-emerges, only to process along exactly the same route, mothers nervously smiling, hand-held toddlers gawping, in a jerky line of pastel pinks and blues, this time to the flashing and clacking of cameras. And this was about all the celebration on today's agenda. Time now for some serious reminders of the crucifixion, out of a 1955 edition of the Baptist Hymnal, published in Nashville, Tennessee. Perhaps this last fact explained why these hymns were so easy to sing along with – three-chord worship, it was. And now, a solo from a pubescent choirgirl accompanied by a boogie box: yes, it was karaoke time in the house of God; organ and drum-machine cooked away as she attempted a hymn of redemption, easy-listening style; but the girl was woefully under-rehearsed and kept having to stop and then start again, forgetting words and hitting bum notes. However, she got a round of applause at the end, and looked much relieved to have finished. This performance enhanced the impression of fear and lack-of-confidence already installed by the mothers-and-babies parade. But now, after a sufficiently humbling prayer, it was time for instruction: a reading and a sermon, and from who else but St Paul, the Baptists' main man and *Gauleiter*. Nuremberg stood up and discoursed upon the importance and significance of the resurrection, using the tangle of circular logic that is 1 Corinthians 15. It was a sober, un-fired performance, during which Ffarington began making copious notes on the back of an envelope which later turned out to be a detailed rebuttal of each point made.

After this, the choir gave a pretty decent rendition of the spiritual *Were You There (When They Nailed Him to the Cross)?* And then came the grand finale, when Pastor Nuremberg announced that we the congregation were going to have our picture taken. 'Everybody here's looking so fine,' he declared, 'and I just know you're going to want to order copies of this photograph, just so's to be able to say, "I was there." You know it's a great thing to be able to say "I was there." Yes, even when that old atom bomb drops, it'll be great to be able to say, "I was there." That's right.'

When the atom bomb drops, indeed. And he meant it. I've got my copy of the picture: ninety-seven decent, respectable folks looking out from their pews, smiling, sort-of-eagerly awaiting that old blinding flash of Armageddon.

Nuremberg was at the door as we all filed out. I shook his hand and said, 'Nice choir you have.' He gave me that hard smile again and said, 'Ay-men.' Ffarington said, 'Thank you.' Nuremberg said, 'Y'all come back.'

I looked at this guilt-mongering, narrow-minded, interfering, righteous son-of-a-dog, a person whose mission was to make men uncomfortable and women look like fools, and I thought, not in this lifetime.

Back in Sandpoint, further out of town there was indeed the usual eighties' shopping centre with its K-Mart, Radio Shack and J. C. Penney. The Safeway, however, was back at the edge of the old town. Here we discovered one thing more about American coffee. The good news was that the store had a wide selection of beans, some of good strong variety, and a mill there to grind them with. The bad news was that amongst the beans on sale were various luridly flavoured varieties such a strawberry, hazelnut, blackcurrant and peach; everything but cinnamon in fact; and the worst news was that the grinder reeked of their sickly odours. After I'd put a batch of high-roast Colombian through I was aghast to discover it was polluted by the said stink. Discreetly I had to feed three batches through the mill in order to flush out the hostile essences, lay them aside, and carry the fourth away – and even this smelled like a Swiss chocolate shop. Would we ever get a good cup of coffee in the US? Not even in the north-west, where Agent Cooper had found just such a brew in the homely diner at Twin Peaks? Then it dawned on me. This had been director Lynch's message all along: *Twin Peaks* was a world of total fantasy; why, it even had good coffee.

Twin Peaks – something nasty in the woods. By mid-week the pair of us had both discovered something unpleasant in the woods by our camper, where we regularly went to void our bowels. And the something was that we could not. We were both inexplicably blocked. There was no apparent reason for this: we were stuffed silly with fibre and fruit. We were also drinking that Safeway coffee ... but could it be some heinous blocking agent that I'd failed to flush from the grinder? Curious, and uncomfortable. We lay abed nights with aching insides, listening to the distant high-pitched howls of coyotes.

Were we constipated? Does the bear shit in the woods? There were bears around here alright, we'd seen their droppings. One evening we took Clark's canoe out. The canoe was very low in the water, thanks to our handicap of half-a-dozen unexpelled meals. And we constantly had to fend off an irritating cloud of flies who came along for the paddle, and we had to do this gently, for the slightest rocking of the canoe threatened to waterlog us. It's hard to fight off flies in slow motion. But once a couple of dorks in a powerboat had been unintentionally seen off by the strange gestures we were making, bizarrely threatening as they must have appeared, a great quiescent solitude settled over this huge lake, which is forty miles long and up to five miles wide, and the setting sun gave the impression of floating on an ocean of flat, liquid gold; definitely one for the brochures. It was then that we spotted a hunched, black figure shambling across a distant meadow and finally disappearing into some trees. Charming as it was to spot a bear, it was galling to reflect on what it would now be doing in those woods.

On the Friday afternoon the six of us drove over to Bob and Darlene Springer's place, which was a few miles out of Sandpoint at the foot of a mountain, set back from a narrow highway and surrounded by big pine forest. Bob was a builder by trade and he'd done this one himself, again from local lumber, but the effect he went for was your three-storey giant log cabin complete with moose antlers on the wall, and a deck which ran round the upper floor and was overhung by the tops of conifers. Up here we climbed, and went in to settle ourselves in a living room which had super-cumulo-nimbus chairs and sofas, and a giant altarpiece of a wall unit that held thousands of bucks' worth of hifi as well as a TV with a screen the size of a billboard. Little Carrie immediately went off to change into one of the many outfits she had brought with her and emerged soon afterwards in a pink tutu and paraded herself around. Selma Springer served everyone canapés and gargantuan gin-and-tonics. She had just had her first day back at school and was disappointed that she wasn't able to take up French as she'd intended, the reason being that the school had suddenly not been able to afford a French teacher. She told us what she'd have to learn instead: 'Musical Appreciation,' she said disgustedly. Imagining what it was like to be force-fed the classics, I sympathized. Was there no chance of her doing another language, Spanish or Japanese maybe? Nope. No other language on the curriculum. I asked her mother if this worried her at all. It didn't. 'Well, her older sister did French,' said Darlene, as if that somehow made up for it.

It turned out that Bob and Darlene were originally from Los Angeles, California. And a picture was produced: the pair of them, *circa* 1970, standing on a nondescript bare brown hilltop. Bob looked even more like Fat Freddie than he did now – if you looked closely you could see the spirals in his eyes; and Darlene was a slimmer version of her present self, with flared jeans, waist-length hair and eyes that resembled two whirlpools. Ten years ago they had joined the ever-increasing band of folk emigrating from California for a quieter, smog-free life in the north-west. Down in the Golden State there were still thirty million people suffering smog, 'quake, forest fire and social unrest for their slice of the polluted pie; the hopefuls were pouring in as fast as the disillusioned were leaving.

After a while we went outside to explore the Springers' enormous garden, and Darlene showed me around the vegetable patch. As I was admiring some very fat squashes and sumptuous stands of corn, I got a call from across the lawn – beyond where the kids were tossing a football around – from Clark and Bob, who were standing in the doorway of a small outhouse. I went over and joined them inside the hut, where they were surreptitiously indulging in reefer like a pair of miscreant schoolboys. This was beginning to look like something of a syndrome with American husbands. As the joint went round I was informed of the plant's pedigree.

If there's one thing I find more tedious than a script in a ring-binder called *Socrates,* it's talking of the origins of whatever I'm putting into my system at a given time. I don't enjoy drinking with beer-bores obsessed with specific gravity, and I care nothing for the origins of a glass of wine. At least tobacco smokers (barring pipemen droning on about flue-cureds versus semi-brights) are the one variety of drug-takers who never indulge in this habit; they obviously have more important things to worry about, like heart disease and premature death. (I have, however, always been curious to know what it was like to smoke the original tobacco, *Nicotiana rustica*, the stuff that native American and Mexican Indians used to get high on, and against which King James of England issued his *Counterblaste,* banning the substance and threatening smokers with excommuncation. Since then tobacco products have been made with *Nicotiana tabacum,* a much milder strain they found on Tobago in the West Indies; but the wheel goes round, and smokers are once again being threatened with excommuncation.) I stayed in that hut long enough to learn that this marijuana had been grown somewhere indoors in a vast artificially lit concrete silo, and that this was how growers in the States were now defeating the efforts of the helicopter brigades; but when talk turned to prices and stories of famous-highs-I-have-had and so forth, I bowed out and left the boys to it. I joined the women up on deck, and here a certain tension was in the air. Rosey said she didn't care for the men's adolescent behaviour, fooling around in the woodshed while the women were supposed to hang around in the background taking care of kids and domestic details. 'What's the matter?' Darlene snapped back. 'You wanna live in your man's shadow or something?' She was already clearly pissed off with her husband's behaviour – there had been things to get straight, kids to organize, decisions to be made about where we would go to eat this evening – and she'd already been telling him to get his ass in gear, but she didn't like having these matters underlined by an interloper. It was the only spirited comment I was to hear her make.

Things eventually got slowly organized. Selma was left minding the little ones (Carrie was already in her fourth outfit of the evening) and the rest of us drove into Sandpoint. At the first restaurant we tried, a flash-looking place by the lakeside, there was a little scene when Clark had a set-to with its very camp *maître d',* who had apologized for not having any tables and suggested that next time we try booking ahead. Clark seemed to think this was outrageous; it was clearly even worse than being booked for doing 90 on a narrow built-up highway. He let the man have a stream of inarticulate abuse before we coaxed him out of the place. 'I never liked that asshole anyway,' said Clark. Walking a few blocks in the direction of our second choice, Clark spotted a distant parked police car, which caused him to jump up and down and give it the finger: 'Fucking *cops*, ha, ha!'

We ended up at a quiet little place called The Cupboard, where we had a small back room to ourselves. It was a modest, arty eaterie run by some young people known to our hosts. As we installed ourselves and ordered wine, I looked at the pictures hung around the walls: done by local artists and bearing price tags, they were mostly run-of-the-mill landscapes. It was then I saw the duck. It was a very large duck, executed in felt-tip pen, using every possible colour there was in the K-Mart stationery section. It had a ribbon round its neck and a price tag that said five hundred dollars. It was Katie's work. Something told me this was going to be our last night in Idaho, and I swiftly downed two glasses of wine.

The food was average and the conversation was piecemeal. It was hard to get anything going. Bob and Clark, well blasted, were huddled together in their own private world. They were obviously very much in love. Katie and Darlene held a series of long, localized conversations with the various passing staff. I was irritated with this town. I didn't want to be here. I now knew that I didn't particularly care for these people and that the feeling (especially *vis-à-vis* Clark and Darlene, the two dominant males of this circle) was getting to be mutual. Well now, what could I have done at this point? Left immediately for a motel? Spoken up and shared my feelings that there were some mutual attitude problems to be resolved in a loving context? Given a speech denouncing the compromises Katie had made (as she had confided to us) by bearing Clark's children, running his home and putting up with 'everybody calling my husband an asshole' for the sake of this so-called paradise? Suggest that Clark and Bob quit the charade, out themselves and shack up together quickly before Bob found himself stabbed in the back and pushed overboard one day by a Commander caught in the throes of erotic guilt? And perhaps, too, that Katie and Darlene get it on and teach themselves French in bed? Not me. At one point Katie confided to me that Darlene had 'Indian blood' in her. I'd heard this before from people – why not?

I also suspected, maybe unfairly, that for many of them it was wishful thinking. Katie's eyes widened as she explained to me that the Indians were 'very spiritual people'.

I imagined that I could smell something called Romanticizing Oppressed Racial Groups Whom We Are Really Rather Afraid Of. Europeans had the same thing about gypsies: fabulous, free, mystical, magical, but not on our land, brother. But some gypsy blood, yes, that was alright. Slice them up and rape their daughters. And then, the blood being *on* them, they claim that it's *in* them. It was like having some reformed Nazi tell you, yes, she had some Jewish blood in her: 'Ja, well the Jews you know are very spiritual people ...' Does one gather spiritual strength from a sacrificial slaughter? Obviously so, by definition. We slit the throat, drink the blood and consume the flesh; thus we take on the spirit and the attributes of the victim. Some of us do it every Sunday with the god Jesus.

And here was Katie telling me that Darlene was supposed to be 'spiritual'. So, with sufficient tact to stun a buffalo, I said, 'Yeah, but there are plenty of stupid Indians, too. Like in any race.' And I then wondered aloud whether 'spirituality' was learned or innate.

Katie was looking at me with a bemused expression. She asked me to explain. I stumbled on in an attempt to de-glamorize the Indian nations, pointing out some of their mistakes such as signing treaties with the white man that weren't worth the paper they were written on, Uncle-Tomming for Custer, and so forth, until I realized that Katie's eyes had glazed over and her smile was on automatic pilot.

Across the table, talk had got around to our hosts' impending boating holiday in Grenada. They'd been planning the trip for some time. Curious, I asked how big the island was. Nobody knew. Well, where exactly was it situated, then – near Cuba? Nearer South America? Again, nobody knew. I was a little startled, but not that startled; after all, Clark had just written a whole movie script set off Costa Rica and he knew zero about that place, too. 'What!' I exclaimed. 'Your country had a high-profile invasion of this place not so long ago and you don't even know where it is or who runs it?' No one came back at me. No one said, 'Yeah, and we kicked some good Commie butt that day,' or 'How about you draw *us* a map of the Falklands, smartass?' My exclamation was ignored as a haze of incoherence settled over proceedings. Later, as we made our way out of The Cupboard, and thinking that The Closet might be a more appropriate name, I was conscious of some extremely hostile vibrations coming at me from a couple of the staff – I didn't discover until much later that I had forgotten to leave a tip on the credit card slip. I was fast becoming *non grata* around Sandpoint.

Even more incoherent by now, our party somehow ended up at the marina, and aboard Bob's boat, chugging out to the middle of the lake. It was a clear night, the water still as glass, the stars everywhere in the sky. The engine was cut and we drifted to a standstill. Then Clark and Bob decided it was time to do some sailing. The fact that there wasn't enough wind to drive an ant's fart did not deter them. They rushed around putting the sail up, and then waited. Nothing happened. Katie and Darlene went down into the cabin. Still nothing happened. Not a breath of wind. The boys seemed delighted, nevertheless: 'Hey, Commander!' – 'Hey, Captain!' The minutes passed. Someone turned on the stereo. I watched the lights of Sandpoint glimmering in the distance, and the lights from a sawmill glowing green by the lakeside. Beer and reefer were passed round. Someone turned off the stereo. Then, there was a puff of wind. The boat advanced at a steady fraction of half a knot. This caused great excitement from the boys: 'We're moving, Commander – heh, heh, heh!' – 'That's right Captain, we're moving, hey!' We moved for three minutes or so before the breeze died. Some minutes later it sprung up with equal vehemence, accompanied by equal delight from the two sailors; and so it went, stop–go in this manner for about an hour before everyone but the two officers expressed boredom, and we then chugged back to landfall. On the way it struck me that for someone who claimed to be a well-seasoned salt, Clark was unduly excited by this piece of recreation. Was he really an old Caribbean hand (hence his daughter's name?), or was it just fantasy? And could he tell the difference, anyway?

Waking up the next morning, not without a trace of hangover, I unzipped a canvas flap and looked out through the screen to the cottonwoods, the wide green lawn with its vegetable patch, and across to the house. More and more I'd come to feel like some naturalist hunkered in his hide and observing a peculiar variety of native fauna. I'd once read a book by a Cambridge anthropologist about her studies of English gypsies: for the purposes of her work this scientist had lived in a caravan at the edge of the travellers' camp and reported from this base. The present situation was looking uncomfortably familiar. Uncomfortable because we had not entered into the same contract as the anthropologist. We were supposed to be friends. But any pretension of friendship, especially with Clark Fournier, would now be a sham. We couldn't progress beyond mere politesse, and even that was getting strained. It was clearly time to leave.

As it happened, we were run out of town. I was already planning our route when we had a visit from Katie, upset and angry. We were accused of insulting behaviour, and of playing 'mind games'. After we had talked for a while, she was somewhat reassured, but declared that Clark wanted us gone as soon as possible. 'Clark wants his space,' she explained. No problem at all, we said. 'I'd like you to stay,' she said, 'but my family comes first. And it's about Harmony.'

We asked if we could have a word with Clark before we left, to leave the air a little clearer, but this was not on. Clark, somewhat at variance with his declared persona, was running shy of us now. Nevertheless, there was reconciliation with Katie – there were even hugs all round.

It took us a couple of hours to pack and clean up the trailer. During this time the kids were conspicuously absent from the vicinity, although they were to be seen playing closer to the house. We were obviously now a corruptive influence and strictly out of bounds for the duration. Of Clark there was no sign at all, although his car was here. Perhaps he was busy writing a story of two English folk who arrive in a Japanese car and take his wife and children hostage. No end of heroic deeds could flow from such a scenario. But Tom and his sister did actually muster up the courage to approach us, once we were all loaded up and sat in the car and about to start up and go. They stood twenty yards away under the trees, holding hands. 'Are you going?' Tom called out. 'Yes,' we nodded. 'Why?' asked Tom. What do you say to a couple of innocents caught in crossfire? We'd had some good times with them in the past week. It was galling to have to bow to the proprietorial convention between parent and child, and not to get out of the car and make a humane farewell of it. But for all we knew Clark might be jealously observing this scene from somewhere with a pistol in his hand and a copy of *Chronicle of a Death Foretold* in his pocket. 'We just have to go,' we said, and we waved, and they waved back, and we lurched off along the track. The kids ran up to the gatepost, from where they watched us gain the road. A half-mile on, we spotted Katie sitting sketching in the middle of a hayfield. We stopped, and waved a brief goodbye, and Katie waved back.

There's an expression – to live in your own private Idaho. It's easy to be private in this state. It's mountainous, underpopulated, and it doesn't really lead anywhere. We had found amicable folk here, like the young fellow at a gas station who'd never seen a South Carolina plate in his life (tag plates and bumper stickers serve as useful conversation-openers since they speak of origins, colleges attended, political views, etc.); 'You folks are a long way from home,' this exchange had begun, typically, and it ended with his offer of serious dollars for our vehicle. But beyond this initial friendliness there was a formidable reserve. These people appeared to have their backs against the wall, squeezed up here in the panhandle, pressed against the Canadian border (Canadians were wild and untrustworthy – this was the general opinion we observed), huddled between the Bitter Roots and Spikeheart City. They looked out at the rest of America and the world beyond with suspicion and they disliked being probed by visitors. They made the Deep South look extrovert and cosmopolitan by comparison.

And so, fuelled by the conviction that these isolated backwoods must have been the very model for *Twin Peaks*, a community where child-like innocence and dark desires came together in a sleazy, curdled conjunction, I found myself conjuring up a caricature: where Lake Pend Oreille has become a warped version of Walden Pond, populated with subscribers to the Libertarian Party; a place teeming with mean Canadians in glitzy Buicks running whores and narcotics across the border; dotted with churches set up with sinister motives and criminal theologies: race hatred, child abuse, tax evasion ... and where the coffee always tastes of cherry pie. And where every young plaid-shirted lumber worker is Billy Budd and every employer's brain teems with forbidden desires and murderous guilt. And where all the little girls, just like Carrie, were auditioning hard for their part in *The Stepford Wives*.

As for us Brits, we were revealed literally for what we were: completely constipated. The price, perhaps, of outstaying our welcome for the sake of a mercenary exercise in anthropology plus some nice scenery.

5. The Magic of the Mundane

'I have a debt of gratitude towards this stuff,' said the old
gentleman in the blue meat hat as he stirred four spoonfuls of
sugar into his plastic coffee cup – 'See, I was in the navy in World
War II, I served on an LTC, the USS Pittsburgh. We were hit by
the same typhoon as struck the carrier USS Okinawa. Yes, there
was myself and twenty others at sea for five days in a lifeboat till
we finally made it to Iwujima. And you know what kept us alive?
– Lifesavers and Pepsicola. That's all we had. Good ol' sugar!
And the Lord's help of course – couldn't 'a' done it without him.'
And he smiled, raised the beaker in a salute and sipped from its
contents.

We were at a rest area on Interstate 90 near Ritzville, eighty
miles into Washington state. Our acquaintance, a tall, solidly built
man, fair-skinned and blue-eyed, was helping run the free coffee
stand along with his wife and other members of the local Masonic
lodge. There was a fair crowd of rest seekers that afternoon,
milling around under patchy, windblown skies which every few
minutes would drop a light shower of rain across the layby. The
other side of the parking lot an old fellow in a cowboy hat was
being helped from a car, quivering in every limb, and aimed by his
companion in the direction of the coffee stand. Each step took him
half a minute to complete, but it seemed he was determined to
make the trip rather than have the coffee come to him.

Our friend in the meat hat was telling us some of his life story.
Originally from Texas, he'd worked in Oklahoma, then in NYC's
Bronx, where he'd shed his southern accent, and then all up and
down the West Coast, in every trade you could name. One of his
proudest achievements was having been a carpenter on the Grand
Coulee Dam, one of the jewels in the crown of Roosevelt's great
reconstruction programme; and had we visited this place as he

urged us to (it was just fifty miles north of here) we would have known exactly which doors, panels and ceilings were his own handiwork. But I was more interested in his Freemasonry than his carpentry, and the peculiar connections of this Enlightenment philosophy with the United States of America.

Freemasonry, that colourful mixture of theory, symbolism, ritual and conspiracy, emerged in eighteenth-century Europe as a synthesis of strands from many previous occult/scientific traditions – Kabala, Alchemy, Gnosticism, Pythagoreanism, Egyptology, and so forth. These men were particularly opposed to the organized religion of the day, especially Catholicism and its attendant ageing political systems. Individual enlightenment for all was their ideal, unmediated by corrupt priests or decadent monarchies; and their god was a god to match this new age of rationalism: an architect and designer-of-the-universe as opposed to some anthropomorphic white-bearded politician.

The founders of the United States did not go so far as to ban the practice of organized religion in their new nation, but they were careful to keep it clear from the mechanisms of state: 'Congress shall make no law respecting an establishment of religion ...' as the First Amendment kicks off. The USA was founded on ideals of Illuminist Freemasonry. Its founding fathers were Masons: Jefferson was well-versed in esotericism and astrology, Ben Franklin had been a Grand Master of Pennsylvania Lodges and a master of a lodge in Paris. The Great Seal of the US, which these two designed together with John Adams, is a collection of Masonic symbolism; its reverse, to be seen on every dollar bill, shows the pyramid, the all-seeing eye, and the motto *Novus Ordo Seclorum*. This new secular order can be interpreted as meaning a pure, theocratic republic: 'One Nation Under God', with no need for church ... or government? For the Bill of Rights is by and large an instrument designed to protect citizens from the excesses of government; Jefferson is quoted as saying that given the choice between newspapers or government, he would take his chances with newspapers. So, no doubt, would Henry David Thoreau. Given this well-engrained attitude, it's easy to see how policies such as those promoted in America during the eighties, which withdrew funds from public and community projects, could be presented as the politics of non-interference by government, when it was merely a matter of tax cuts for the rich. Not that we have seen the US government interfere less in other areas, especially in its foreign policy. But this too makes Masonic sense: for the two-faced – sorry – double-headed eagle of the Great Seal of the United States is an ancient symbol of the ruler of the globe, the *Rex Mundi*, and an emblem of Scottish Rite Freemasonry. And now, while George Bush's domestic scene was beginning to collapse, both in terms of the economy and voter-support, what was he promoting? – a *Novus Ordo Mundi,* no less.

Coincidences and conspiracies: the stuff of all speculation about secret societies and world domination; the eagle, badge of those old European imperial aspirations from Peter the Great to Franz Joseph to Adolf Hitler ... and if you wanted a Masonic connection between the US and the USSR, why, hadn't Karl Marx himself been an Illuminist Mason? ... and to really stretch things, you could point out that the medieval Shi-ite Muslim Hassan I Sabbah, who from his stronghold in the mountains of Persia launched a system of terrorism still familiar today, was a member of the Lodge of Cairo, whose system of nine-degree initiation is said to be preserved in many contemporary American Masonic groups. So there's your Irangate connection ...

The Mason at the Ritzville coffee stand showed me his rings, and I was struck by a symmetry: on the prairies to one side of the Rockies we had talked murder and conspiracy with Frank; now here, on the prairies to the other side, I was talking to a Mason of the Scottish Rite. And, moreover, there was a theory at large that the Scottish Rite had been involved in the JFK killing. The Scottish Rite was originally an offshoot of the Knights Templar, who were proto-Masons vehemently opposed to the Bourbon Monarchy and the Papacy. They were said to have a slogan which was later to become rather well known – Liberty, Equality, Fraternity. When their leader Jacques de Molay was imprisoned by Philip the Fair and awaiting death at the stake, he is supposed to have set up a number of secret lodges around the fringes of Europe. One of these was said to have been founded at Edinburgh – thus, 'Scottish Rite'. One of its rituals involves the symbolic stabbing of two skulls which represent the Papacy and the Bourbons. Another involves an initiate playing the role of the architect of the ancient temple of Solomon in Jerusalem being 'assassinated' by 'three unworthy craftsmen'.

Now, the Kennedy-assassination theory goes roughly as
follows: JFK was the first and only Roman Catholic president of
the US, and therefore intolerable to a state founded on Masonic
ideals. Dealy Plaza, the site of the killing, was the site of a since-
demolished early nineteenth-century Masonic lodge. The squad
who blew the president's brains out from their spot on the grassy
knoll were three in number and stood for the 'unworthy craftsmen'
already mentioned. (There is a famous news photo of 'three
hoboes' arrested near the knoll immediately after the killing, one
of whom is supposed to look like famous CIA man E. Howard
Hunt, later notorious for his role in Watergate. These three were
mysteriously released almost immediately by the Dallas police,
never to be seen or heard of again.) The theory draws on other
varieties of wacky coincidence, but that is the bare bones of it – a
ritual king-killing by CIA Masons with Lee Harvey Oswald as the
fall guy. Frank would probably not have been interested in the
event's mystic trappings, but he and many others would go for the
basic CIA-conspiracy scenario.

I asked our friendly Mason if he and his mystic brothers
involved themselves in politics at all. Naturally enough, he gave a
friendly denial. 'We're basically a charity organization. Our lodge
even admits Jews – and blacks. We've had a falling-out with other
lodges who don't see eye to eye with us on this one.' They even
had Catholics in the fraternity, he claimed. Catholics! Whatever
next? Women? His wife, a neat blonde in jeans and sneakers, told
us she was in one of the women's orders, Eastern Star. Rosey
asked if they accepted men. Yes, they did, but no, there was no
reciprocation – the traditional male lodges remained just so, as her
husband confirmed. Any reason for this? – 'None that I've ever
seen written down, Ma'am – and so far because of our status as a
religion no one's been able to sue.'

Our friend didn't mind talking a bit of politics, however: he said
he saw a lot of changes coming to these parts when the hispanic
immigrants began getting the vote and making the changes they
wanted – better health care, education and other socialistic ideals.
These people obviously disturbed him somewhat, but he would not
be drawn on whether the results would be good or bad: 'It'll take
five or ten years. It'll be interesting. We'll just have to wait and

see.' He then used the 'hippies' as an example of what he meant: 'They were rebellious once, but after a while, you see, they came to realize they wanted just what everyone else does – a family, a car ... and pretty soon they all rejoined the fold.'

The fold wouldn't ever be the same again, though. Twenty-five years ago, if your average American had stood up and questioned the nation's eating habits, or talked ecology, or suggested that the Vietnam war maybe wasn't such a good thing, or expressed a fondness for loud rock music, he or she would have been asked where they were getting those crazy revolutionary hippy ideas from.

The Mason's wife then told us about the time Mount St Helens, 150 miles west of here in the Cascades, had erupted back in 1980 and the lethal ash clouds had drifted east. 'It was spectacular,' she said. 'The sky was dark as night and filled with what looked like thousands of curls of smoke. We were in church at the time. We jumped – the Reverend jumped! But it was truly fantastic, and the farmers who complained about crops being ruined have had bumper harvests ever since; see, that ash was full of minerals!'

As the old fellow in the cowboy hat finally made it to the coffee stand we took our leave. A mile or so up the road, where I-90 veered due west towards the Cascade Mountains and, beyond these, Seattle, we turned on to US 395, past the little town of Lind, where a signboard proclaimed 'Drop in on Lind – Mount St Helens did!', and from here began a gradual, sixty-mile descent towards the Columbia River, sticking to our south-west course. The sky cleared and the sun, though low in the sky, began to roast us. We were driving through vast tracts of open prairie, covered with purple sagebrush and suffused with golden light. Clumps of tumbleweed bowled across the empty highway and, off to our right, the railroad tracked our course as every so often we'd find ourselves drawing past a seemingly endless line of slow-rolling freight wagons laden with as much myth and song and legend as they were with goods: every time we passed one I'd hear Sonny Terry's harmonica wailing, or Ry Cooder singing 'Boomer's Story', or The Persuasions doing 'There's a Train Coming', or Bob Dylan singing about a long-distance train crawling through the rain, or I'd see Jack London, John Steinbeck and Woody Guthrie huddled inside a blind wagon singing 'Bound for Glory' with a young unshaven Henry Fonda joining in the chorus. This was the freight train for Americans: a slow, relentless, immensely heavy procession, as inevitable and irresistible as the Coming of the Kingdom; a ticket to the Great Beyond; its mournful, discordant horns wailing through the night across the great wilderness; and up in the shadowy cab its invisible driver, the Great Engineer of the Universe, leading his people on, out of the dustbowl, away from home and misery, across to the promised land in the west. Occasionally, though, I'd see Casey Jones up there in the cab – not the coke fiend from the Grateful Dead's song, but the good guy from the old TV series, his chubby face smiling and aglow beneath his pinstriped cook's hat.

Near Pasco we crossed the Columbia River and then went up and over the grassy expanses of the Horse Heaven Hills, a great twenty-mile-wide bluff formed by the Columbia as it makes a giant hairpin before finally setting its course west to the ocean. So we were soon crossing the Columbia a second time, and at Umatilla on the Oregon line, an exhausted-looking township full of motels and cheap trailer parks, we called it a day. Umatilla looked as though it had just dragged itself three thousand miles across the continent before collapsing here, weak and weary. But its scraggy strip of beaten-up buildings looked beautiful against the colourful sunset. And nothing compliments an American sundown more than the glow of fresh-lit neon. And nothing complimented the end of that heady day's journey more than the stupendous vacation-of-the-bowels that we were both finally able to treat ourselves to.

From Umatilla the Columbia flows due west for a hundred and fifty miles to the Willamette valley, cutting through the Cascade range – the last obstacle before the Pacific – before taking a north-west course to the ocean. The half-million settlers who took this route along the last stage of the Oregon Trail in the great period of emigration between 1840 and 1870 had no transcontinental railroad to speed their journey; in fact most of them did the two-thousand-mile-plus hike on foot, maybe pulling a handcart or pushing a wheelbarrow. At least, they started out on foot; the prevailing idea that most of them were in covered wagons is possibly because those who actually made it this far did have better means of transportation. Or it could stem from confusion with the Santa Fe Trail further to the south, originally opened up as a trade route to the south-west, which featured great convoys of wagons – although the teams of mules and oxen which pulled them rarely feature in the Hollywood version of things, which tends to stick to horses. I can't remember a single episode of *Wagon Train*, the fifties' TV series that drilled the westward-ho legend so thoroughly into the minds of the post-war generation, which dared feature any four-legged hoofed creature more lowly than a (well-fed) pony, unless it was a herd of stampeding cattle. And tramping across the Rockies on worn shoe-leather was not seen as a very heroic image to the myth makers of the day. In the same way, you won't see any road movies, from *Five Easy Pieces* and *Vanishing Point* to *Thelma and Louise*, which dare feature their all-American heroes dashing about in anything as lowly as a little Japanese car.

Interstate 80 hugs the foot of the steep cliffs of the Columbia Gorge for close on a hundred miles. The views are gigantic, from the vertiginous canyon walls of yellow basalt, the ever-widening river, and the approaching mountains, to the sight of Mount Hood itself, a vast snow-capped cone: for a moment I imagined that the Japs had gone and imported Fujiyama itself to northern Oregon.

The early pioneers stopped at The Dalles – they'd often rafted the river to this point – to load up for the last seventy miles from here to what is now Portland, on the Willamette. We stopped to gas up and look around the Salvation Army store for sneakers, and admire yet another little town centre frozen in time – or rather baked in time, given the fierce heat of that day. Its old red- and yellow-brick buildings made the place seem archaeologically ceramic. Its main street café hadn't been refurbished since the days of Eisenhower; and at each table was a little wall-selector for the jukebox, most of whose tunes were at least thirty years old (as were the local attitudes – much low whispering when a group of hispanics came in and sat down). But, leaving town, the present quickly caught up with us. The reason why the centres of so many rural American towns remain so pristine is because, as the towns grow, they have so much surrounding space to expand into. There is no need for wholesale European-style demolition and redevelopment – whenever you want to put up something new you buy a chunk of land on the outskirts and build it there. And out there, away from the cute beauty of the old courthouse squares and nineteenth-century grids, is another kind of beauty, that of the commercial strips of the post-war era: the sprawl of retail and business development dotted along every main road out of town; lowrise blocks surrounded by parking lots, strung with overhead telegraph- and power-lines and traffic signals, and announced by lofty signboards: the banks, supermarkets, car dealerships, restaurants, malls, gas stations, and the rest. This beauty is above all a supremely functional one – it works perfectly. Traffic flows with ease, there is plenty of space, stores are uncrowded and relaxed, horizons are wide both inside and out, and there is a peculiar quietude which suffuses the environment. The objection that most aestheticists have to this quintessential American scene is founded on a set of archaic, backward-looking assumptions which hold that a) advertising communications should be discreet; b) power cables should be invisible; c) telegraph poles are ugly; d) parking lots are ugly; e) the only good landscape is one by Constable or, at a stretch, Andrew Wyeth; f) a shopping centre must have some trees somewhere; and g) Americans are pedestrians. Wrong on every count. And, what's more, it will be those who have been passed the torch of this ultra-conservationist, nostalgic ethos who will be calling – equally wrongheadedly – for the preservation of this very landscape once a future style has superseded it. But for now the strip remains, in its quiet and banal grandeur, the perfect compliment to all those mountains, trees, plains, lakes and prairies – which themselves can get mighty tiresome after a while. In times off from the grotesque, the fantastic and the unusual, there is enlightenment amongst concrete, brick, drive-thru banking and Pepsi machines; there is the magic of the mundane. American culture has never been loath to celebrate this magic; indeed, it has played a crucial role in arts and letters since before the middle of the twentieth century. A quick survey will highlight this love affair with the banal.

Until his death in 1992, John Cage was the doyen of new American music, and ever since he came to prominence in the 1940s his works have been saturated with a worship of the everyday; he started off using brake drums and spanners as percussion instruments, and jamming piano strings with nuts and bolts; his '4'33"', in which a pianist sits at the keyboard for that amount of time and does nothing, means that all you hear are the common little sounds all around you: coughs, shuffling-in-seats, the humming of the air-conditioning, a car rushing by outside; and many more of his pieces feature the output from randomly tuned radios – fragments of news programmes, sports shows and other bits of music. Cage's aesthetic owes a great deal to Marcel Duchamp, who was the first to exhibit such things as ready-made urinals, bottle-racks and chocolate grinders; and Duchamp himself, though born in France, was a long-time New Yorker by the time he died. Both men made their careers out of a celebration of the ordinary. Cage's oft-repeated statement is 'let sounds be themselves'. He was none-too-fond of overplanning and would probably have applauded anyone who wanted to stick poles and wires and supermarkets exactly where they liked. He also adored old Henry David Thoreau, and extended the latter's political anarchy to the cultural field. Cage has influenced a whole crowd of younger musicians of whom the most well known are probably Steve Reich, Terry Riley and Philip Glass; and their trademark has been repetition – *ad infinitum* – of simple themes, which is the musical equivalent of eating every meal of the day, for seven days, at a different McDonalds; depending on how you approach this, the result can be either enlightenment or cardiac arrest. Pop musician David Byrne has also followed the same road. An early Talking Heads album is called *More Songs About Buildings and Food*; and Byrne has written eloquently of the glories of shopping malls and Pizza Huts. And just as nearly every American pop and blues song is replete with names of towns, highways and brands of gasoline, the same goes for the country's literature. You don't slip into a shirt, you put on a Ben Sherman; you don't make a scotch on the rocks, you pour yourself a J&B and take some ice from the Westinghouse; you don't get into a car, you climb into your Ford, Chevy or Buick; and you then proceed to a confrontation whereby you don't blow someone away with a pistol, you blast them with a Colt Magnum. Thus everyday objects are glorified by brand name; and this attitude reaches its apotheosis in a book like *American Psycho*, where every single object is fetishized by its label.

The clearest example of all this homage to the humble is in the work of Andy Warhol, who gave god-like status to the soup can;

you can say that his work is ironic, just as Jasper Johns's American flags and painted numbers, and Roy Lichstenstein's enlargements of comic-strip art, and even Robert Rauschenberg's collages of everyday junk – but irony is in the mind of the beholder, and you can be sure that there are millions of Americans who have bought these images without seeing the joke, if any joke were intended. Edward Hopper, who glorified the ordinary with his loving depictions of the exterior elevations of the most ordinary buildings, was certainly not joking: *Gas Station*; *Nighthawks*; *Usherette*; *Office Building, New York City*; and all the rest, are heroic attempts to glorify the normal, simply by rendering them in a heightened, supra-normal light. No one could magnify a piece of brickwork or a filing cabinet like Hopper, and it was from him and Duchamp that Warhol and the rest took their cue.

As for American TV, this is a self-evident case of heightened banality; whereas Hollywood sometimes tries bravely to break this mundane mould and deal with the mythic – a copy of Joseph Campbell always in the Director's pocket – unfortunately coming a cropper by insisting on those happy endings. (*Twin Peaks* failed as TV because it tried to bring the pretensions of cinema to the everyday world of television.)

This adulation of the ordinary is by no means a bad thing. At its best it implies a very spiritual celebration of even the most humble articles of creation. It has a lot of the Buddhist in it: God moving amongst the pots and pans and the trivia of daily existence; and again it's very Blakeian – heaven in a grain of sand, or a soup can. The problem arises when day-to-day existence becomes too intolerable even to be considered for a moment in this light. And when daily life becomes this desperate – as it is for millions of Americans who have never had the luxury of contemplating the best of their country's art – and when each moment of existence is just a shithouse struggle on the crappy side of the tracks, this is when good old monotheistic religion steps in and craps things up even further by playing on the anxieties of life and the fear of death and emphasizing the very opposite of the mundane: You too can have an eternal holiday from all this misery, say the preachers – just do what we tell you and give us your money. That so many of America's powerful preachers give not a fig for the holiness of ordinary existence is only too evident from the way in which they ordinary existence is only too evident from the way in which they have been shown to conduct their own daily lives, i.e. in a brazen, hypocritical squalor. But this serves only to reinforce their message. In the long run, the well-publicized 'sins' of the Baakers and Falwells and their ilk simply strengthen the notion that all worldly activity has been corrupt since the expulsion from Eden and there's nothing to be done about it save to cry a few maudlin tears, pray for forgiveness and take a chance on a better life in the Great Beyond. This is one good reason why the miseries of narcotics and guns and racism *et al.* are not being seriously confronted. The religious leaders – particularly the white ones – have too much invested in lawlessness and despair and plain, ordinary boredom. Their accusatorial militance would be lost without it. And what was interesting to watch in their televisual sermons night after night, from motel to motel, was the way the Christian Right, always actively seeking Armageddon, shifted its focus as the threat from the fast-disintegrating Soviet Union was seen to be receding. Now the scenario was no longer in the starry, warry skies in a battle between righteous republic and evil empire. Now Armageddon would be right where the Bible said it would be. We could forget about Russians now; Israelis, Christians and Muslims were destined to blow themselves to hell and drag everyone else with them, as the twenty-dollar video would make even clearer, folks. And if you didn't sign up with Jesus you'd miss out on the company of the chosen few who would be rapidly airlifted out of the mess and straight up to heaven faster than a Sikorsky from the roof of a besieged embassy. These are the cataclysmic obsessions of the men whose everyday life is a round of financial extortions and unhappy little sexual indulgences. But I'm glad they're on TV, because if they weren't able to loose their puerile fantasies like this they'd be running into shopping malls and mowing down passers-by with rounds of automatic fire. Instead they're investing in world destruction. That's how much *they* care for the mundane.

We left the Columbia at Portland, raced through the peak hour traffic on its elevated freeways, and headed straight for the Pacific on Highway 18. Traffic soon thinned out and then we were running on a near-deserted road over the gentle slopes of the coastal range. By now the Datsun had clocked up five thousand miles and it was running as well as ever. Except for the clutch business back in Pennsylvania, it hadn't generated a single problem, which was more than we could have hoped for. But by now its two drivers were feeling the need for a more conventional kind of holiday: a room by the beach in a little seaside town would do fine, and, according to the map, US 101, which trickles all the way down the Oregon coast to California, was dotted with just such communities.

We hit lucky with the first town we came to: Lincoln City (pop. 5,000), an unpretentious kind of place, strung along five miles of coast road with the ocean on one side and the pine forest on the other: a straggle of timber buildings, small motels, modest little shops and restaurants. And miles of wide, white-sanded beach, and cliffs that rose and fell in gentle undulations, and out there the sun dropping over the ocean; whilst along the little seafront esplanade fat brown juvenile gulls hustled the few late-season visitors for scraps of food. Lincoln City was modest in the extreme, but it made two claims to fame: first, in true American style, it boasted the World's Shortest River – this being a stream which dribbles from a lake on one side of the highway, under a bridge and thence across the beach in glistening rivulets; secondly, Lincoln City was the Kite Capital of the Pacific Coast – a slightly more substantial title. Since we had acquired the knack of arriving just too late or too early for local events – the Pumpkintown Festival in Pickens County, the Jackson rally at Hartford, and a string of others across the country – we easily hardened ourselves to the fact that we were a week early for the big kitefest here; but it didn't matter much because out on the beach was one continuous kite show, all day, every day. There were the familiar modest diamond-shaped kites flown by little children, and there were the larger triangular kites handled in acrobatic formations, soaring and swooping and whipcracking as they made their sudden dips and turns; but these were dwarfed by a cluster of candy-coloured monsters flown on stationary lines, hundreds of feet into the air – enormous open-ended cylinders painted with spiral patterns, twirling slowly along their axes, streamers flickering in the vigorous north-westerly wind, suspended up there like fantastic species of monstrous tropical fish, big as barrage balloons, their heavy lines staked securely into the sand. Away from the beach, the seafront shops were adorned with kites in all shapes and sizes; you could buy a kite-version of every kind of fish and bird – and, needless to say, the most popular of the smaller varieties was the Great American Ribboned Duck, bloated and quivering in the wind along countless picket-fences and forecourts. This conflagration of aerial colour made the town as pretty as a suburban commercial strip crowded with blazing McDonalds, Pizza Hut, Days Inn and Shellgas signs. For all this visual noise, though, Lincoln City was a very quiet kind of place. There was no nightlife of any kind. It didn't seem designed to attract the young, for there were no nightclubs, theme parks or amusement parks; there was no family stuff like Krazy Golf, miniature railways, and suchlike – not even a trolley museum; and there were no big hotels or fancy restaurants, and thus a distinct lack of senior citizens in their big beige RVs. In fact there were no resort facilities at all, and the place closed up at 9 p.m. Clearly, all you were supposed to do in Lincoln City was watch the kites, and then gaze in wonder at 'World's Shortest River (length 1,500 ft)'.

So we did both of these, and then went to look for a motel, having decided it would be a good idea to spend a week or so off the road, unbeholden to any hosts, reflecting on the trip so far, and gathering strength for whatever California might have to throw at us. And in a block of pine-tree'd ramshackle streets between the highway and the cliffs we found an L-shaped collection of rooms with a decaying, unlit sign along the roof which featured the name 'Sea Rest' above wave-like curvatures. Draped on the office wall was a bleached-out stars and stripes, but there was no 'American Owned' notice ... and outside was parked a '73 Dodge Dart. This belonged to Harry, a rickety old gentleman in dungarees and meat hat, a friendly fellow who said we could have 7 for a week at a cost of a hundred bucks. And after we'd seen 7 – a small apartment with a fifties' fitted kitchen/lounge and separate bedroom, it seemed like a pretty good deal. It even had a view of the ocean. We'd have to bite one bullet, though: the kitchen table oilcloth was printed with a repeat design of the Great American Ribboned Duck. Just what did Americans see in this white duck, the kind that waddles around the old farmyard with a large family in tow? Their own families, their own backyards, maybe.

Nostalgia for the peasant days when they'd fatten a duck all year and it became one of the family, with a name, and a ribbon round its neck – but what a merry meal it made come winter! Nostalgia for old Europe. In the folk tales of old Europe the duck is not particularly exalted, although it has a cameo role ferrying Hansel and Gretel across the lake to their happy ending; and in a story called *The Vagabond* a duck is mugged by two desperado chickens who force it to pull their cart, but it later takes revenge – great scenario, guys, we'll have Bruce Willis in the part. However, in these tales from the collective roots (the kulaktive unconscious?), more than one duck has its throat cut or belly slit to reveal ... gold, wealth, the source of happiness. This bird seems to suggest the good old ways of thrift, investment and windfall, a safe deposit box on legs. You may be thousands of bucks in hock to a score of finance companies, your Savings & Loan account gone forever, and the view from the condo may be of just another condo in just another edge city; but on the table and on the wall there remains this fat fluffy dream of succulent flesh and a belly full of gold, a pin-up with pinioned wings, sexy as a centrefold. The Great American Duck was perfect for this room too, it suited the character of the place, as did the kitsch framed photograph on the wall above the sofa which depicted a lurid sunset over foaming surf and was overprinted, in the kind of typeface used for Val Doonican albums, with the motto, 'The Lowest Ebb is always the Turning of the Tide.' A comforting tautology. Here was a soundbite George Bush might well use in his continuous claim that the recession was bottoming out. Next to this picture, a small bookshelf held copies of a number of romantic novels and Reader's Digest condensed versions of titles I'd never heard of. The sofa itself was a big orange-based colour-clashing affair straight out of Roseanne Arnold and John Goodman's TV home – all American. We liked Room 7 at the Sea Rest. Tom had been chasing Jerry around here for at least forty years. The only modern thing about the place was the giant TV on a wall-shelf by the window. Upon this Clarence Thomas, who was looking more and more like ITN's reporter and newsreader Trevor MacDonald, was still being grilled by the Congressional committee; 'Pro-lifers' were still beating the shit out of Kansas cops; Jeffrey Dahmer was still making Milwaukee famous; and there were racist attacks up in

Portland. And then there was Jesse Jackson – now a big media star with his own TV debate-show – suddenly declaring that 'What America needs is Perestroika.' This statement ruffled no feathers. All America seemed silently to concur that a process invented by a Soviet Communist party boss was indeed what it needed. But when all the TV socio-economic angst became too much to bear, and all the complacent comedians began to make Morecombe and Wise look as subversive as Saccho and Vanzetti – there was always the distraction of baseball, only ever a channel-hop away. The consolation of sport. I'd been making a side-project out of watching this game and gradually assimilating the rules: I'd even worked out what 'bases loaded' means. Maybe I'd be rooting for teams before the week was out. It was as if we had seven days in a place where we could pretend to be ordinary, unemployed US citizens in a modest little home, watching TV, going to the supermarket, drinking percolated coffee and rooting through junk at the thrift shop.

But there was also the beach. Oregon is relatively unusual in having so many miles of wide, uncrowded, free public beaches to stroll along and watch the Pacific rollers and the pelicans skimming the waves. Striding along these flat sands was not unlike driving the interstates: a steady rhythm and an endless strip of beige in front of me. Baseball was still on my mind. Richard Ffarington had once told me, in his usual ironic tone, that it had been introduced to the country by Russian sailors in the nineteenth century. But I still saw more of the German in it. Was it those square caps; or was there something sadomasochistic and Prussian about all the leather and metal worn by the crouching, masked figure behind the batter? I couldn't put my finger on it. I diverted myself by hunting for sand dollars, those calcified white discs of fossilized sea-creature which were sold in quantity by all the souvenir shops round here. But I couldn't find a single one that wasn't broken. Clearly you had to get up early to find the perfect specimens. Sand dollars. Dollars. A fact flashed out from the recesses of memory: 'Dollar' came from 'Thaler', an early German currency unit named after a certain valley – or *Thal* – where the coin was first minted. Autobahn-like freeways; square caps; German currency. There was something, too, about the way Americans spoke. Not that they all talked with a conspicuously that; it cropped up in odd words, like Dollar itself, or in parts of words, the way for instance final 'd's are pronounced as 't', as in 'secont'. This great country was not what it seemed. The very fact that its people spoke English was deceptive, and made of its otherness more of a mystery. Unlike the other large British colonies, America had made an armed revolution and a complete separation from Britain, and then reconstructed its entire population with two hundred years of immigrations from all over the globe. That Americans still spoke English was a historical accident, an anomaly, a peculiar vestige, like the male breast. I wondered why the founding fathers, having dumped the British political system and established an order based on Illuminist Masonry – an invention of the Bavarian Adam Weishaupt – had not dumped the English language at the same time, along with all the tea they threw into Boston harbour. The fact of an identical tongue had probably made for more misunderstandings between Britain and the USA than any accord it may have provided. For example, on coming to another modern, industrialized country, the Brit might well expect to find a secular nation here, and fondly imagine that that ol' time religion was confined to the 'Bible Belt' of the South. Not so: that *Novus Ordo Seclorum* on the *Thaler* bill means separate, not secular. The country was founded, developed and nourished upon the ideals of Utopian Christianity; and the sustaining myth has been that of a chosen people on a voyage to a better land. The early American hymns are chock full with references to travelling through the wilderness en route to Canaan, to the Great Beyond, and to the New Jerusalem. That's why every other state has a town called Salem; and Arkansas even has a Jerusalem; and there are Canaans, Bethlehems, Hebrons and Jerichos aplenty across the nation. As the people spread out they built themselves a new Holy Land. Like Abraham they moved west in search of milk and honey – or at least non-dairy creamer and nutrasweet – and like Abe they subdued the indigenous population along the way, and then stopped when they reached the coast. They may not have named any towns 'Happy Ending', but they made up for this by building Hollywood and subsequently inventing TV dramas which are still churning out cutely resolved conflicts by the dustbinload. Smaller nations, especially island ones, have a more stoic attitude to misfortune: the Japanese still ones, have a more stoic attitude to misfortune: the Japanese still tend to fall on their swords when all else fails; the British go in for their famous Quiet Desperation with its attendant irony and gallows humour. No Utopias here; but Americans, so often and so rightly described as Utopians, want what they want with a vehemence that can be either supremely practical or extremely childish. On the practical side it has always been a matter of enterprise and travel – a new career in a new town; packing up one's belongings into a U-Haul or a stationwagon and hitting the road for whatever part of the country seems most promising; the North-west, for example, with its cool climate and reputation for being more 'environmentally conscious' is currently riding high in the popularity stakes. As fast as the new immigrants are arriving in California, the Californians are leaving in equal droves for a quieter life in Washington and Oregon. On the childish side, it's simply a matter of robbery, be it corporate or individual, from street hold-ups to the bosses of Chrysler and General Motors giving themselves higher and higher pay rises while their industry crumbles around them. There are no hardships or cruelties that an American believes cannot be mitigated; this is why nearly all their fictions resolve themselves reassuringly, and this is why the British think them naive and are in turn considered cynics: to the Brits, the New Testament is nothing more than a romantic novel that few, even the churchmen, take seriously – their urban culture is way out of tune with such pastoral fantasies; but most of the USA is not nearly so cosmopolitan – apart from the fringe cities of the Great Lakes, the California coast and the eastern seabord, the nation is country-simple, candy-coloured, *Kinder-Küche-Kirche*. Its industrial workers never made the transition from peasantry to proletariat, even though they lived in cities, because there was always that three million square miles of countryside just a short ride away; pasture, wilderness and mountain, all saturated in associations with deistic authority and distant paradise. Besides, it must be hard for a Pennsylvania steelworker to cultivate a hard-edged, European, atheistic fist-clenching workers'-rights attitude if he lives in a town called Bethlehem, or Nazareth. It doesn't have quite the same ring as Dortmund or Middlesbrough. And what means did this urban peasantry now have to support itself, now that it was faced with the crunch of mass lay-offs and an inadequate social welfare system? Just a three-thousand-year-old system of authority and morality that was not up to the task. Granted, they had learned one thing from the nineteenth century – the only piece of Darwinism that all America could be said to agree on: that desperately comforting tautology of 'the survival of the fittest'. America's marvellous and legendary capacity for invention and industry is always going to fail eventually if the bottom line is the law of the jungle and the word of the Pentateuch. Thus reflecting, I tossed away a handful of broken sand dollars in what I imagined was the direction of Japan.

This country was now appearing as one vast museum, from the grand exhibits of past industrial might and spiritual ideas to its domestic architectures: the idyllic lawns, the Tom-And-Jerry interiors, the perfectly preserved '57 Chevy; and, in the minds of its people, an overwhelming collection of nostalgias for everything from sixteenth-century Mennonism to fifties' TV shows like *I Love Lucy;* and an affection for movies like *American Graffiti* and *Back to the Future,* and TV shows such as *Happy Days* and *The Wonder Years*; then there was the obsession with their individual childhoods, whether they came from happy families or 'dysfunctional' ones – those glorious days of white Christmases and the Cold War. And how reluctant was the government to let go, even at this late stage, of the last trappings of that Cold War: it still supported Gorbachev, even as the Soviet Union collapsed irreversibly and as democratically elected leaders were coming to prominence. America needed that big ugly bear-over-there: it had been part of the landscape – nay, part of the family – for forty years; and what would replace it? Why, something in that very dangerous area called the future; *back* to the future was fine – but *forward* to it seemed far too big a risk. They used to say that the future happened first in America – but what was on offer now? Only something called Virtual Reality, that hi-tech system of earphones and helmet-screens that allows the user to play around in an eternal fantasy-land; a closed-circuit of the imagination; a panicked, autistic flight back into the comforting universe of the Self, nourished only by simulacra. 'Make The World Go Away', as Jim Reeves was still singing on jukeboxes and radios across the land; 'America First' as Pat Buchanan, the right-wing presidential contender, was beginning to shout. He'd doubtless get the votes of the Springers and the Fourniers, drifting around on that sailboat on a windless lake in Idaho. That's if they could be bothered to make it to the polling booth.

Hazel and George did all the janitorial business at the Sea Rest, and they lived in the rooms next to ours. They were a couple in early middle-age who had both been married before; the signs of wear and tear showed clearly on their eager, friendly faces. Although Hazel was a God-fearing Christian who involved herself in charity work with drug addicts, she was by no means the puritan type; she and her husband both enjoyed a drink and a smoke, and whenever they had time off they spent it in the gambling dens of ritzy Reno, eight hours' drive away down in Nevada. To get there they used Hazel's van, an '88 Dodge Ram bought new that she proudly showed us over. The vehicle was a rich, royal blue, inside and out. Behind the front seats it was a thick-carpeted lounge, reeking of tobacco and cheap perfume, with a cocktail cabinet, TV on a shelf, and a sofa which could fold out to a double bed. Having dutifully admired the customizing, I asked her how the van performed. 'Oh, don't ask,' she said, not at all mournfully, and then proceeded to reel off a list of all the mechanical troubles it had gone through, and all the times it had been to the garage for almost every kind of complaint you could imagine in a motor vehicle. It was obvious that she had bought a dog – but was she discouraged? Not on your life. She gleefully totalled up the dollars she had spent on it since the warranty ran out: eight thousand bucks it came to, and it clearly didn't bother her at all. 'I just *love* my van,' she said, in her husky eastern tones. 'Couldn't live without it.' Either she was showing off that she had that kind of money to spend, else it was par for the course with an American vehicle. I asked her if she'd considered buying Japanese. 'No,' she said. 'They don't make 'em like this.' No, they certainly didn't.

One morning as we were stepping out for a little trip along the coast, we were confronted by Hazel and George, both wearing worried looks. 'Guys, I'm sorry about your TV,' said Hazel, 'but George'll soon figure out the problem.'

We hadn't a clue as to what she was talking about. What did she mean?

'Well, we noticed you two were in all last night and we saw that the TV wasn't on.'

'We weren't watching it,' said Rosey.

'So what's the matter with it?' said Hazel. 'Maybe it's just the plug. Don't worry. George is good with TVs. He'll figure it out.'

'Yeah,' said George, 'don't you worry. I'll have it working again in no time, else we'll fix you up with a spare.'

We obviously hadn't made ourselves clear; so we had to explain that there was nothing wrong with the TV as far as we knew; and that we hadn't even attempted to watch it last night. It was a few moments before they could come to terms with this startling fact. Hazel had found it easier to accept that we weren't Christians; after all, only a paltry 80 per cent of Americans go to church regularly. But eventually they were reconciled to it and made profuse apologies for their misunderstanding, as if we had been members of some obscure antiquarian religious sect offended by their assumptions.

The other couple we met in Lincoln City were Jack and Dorothy Brady, Irish Americans originally from Chicago, who ran the local second-hand bookshop. We had been impressed by this establishment – it was the first we'd come across on our trip which was not stocked entirely with thrillers, science fiction, metallic-covered seventies' bestsellers, and Bantam editions of *Huckleberry Finn*. Not that their shop was without these genres; but the place had a dusty, mildly academic air too: there were a few reference books, a history section, and some shelves devoted to classical literature. There was also a small area which held such titles as *Kinflicks* and *Fear of Flying:* above these, Dorothy Brady's handwritten sign read 'Naughty Books'.

We got talking to the Bradys in the course of our first mosey around the shop one morning. Like Hazel and George, they'd come out to Oregon a few years back in search of a better quality of life, and they were happy out here: they liked the air, they liked the forests, they liked the ocean, and they liked the comparative quiet. But they too liked to hop down to Reno every once in a while. 'I play all the fruit machines,' said Dorothy, 'while Jack here likes to watch the nudie shows.' Jack, standing by her as she sat at her desk, nodded sagely at this. He was a quiet, slim man in his fifties; his wife was shorter, plumper, and just as matter-offactly agreeable. After giving us some good pointers to a number of restaurants in the area, they gave us a note scribbled on the back of their business card which would later on get us past the security guards and on to a private area of ocean front which comprised of a forested residential area (where the Bradys lived), a golf course dotted with octogenarians dressed in dazzling white and buzzing around on motorized carts, and a spit of beach strewn with giant driftlogs of Oregon pine, upon whose sands the local seal colony basked. It was for the purpose of seal-watching that we had been allowed access to this sanctuary, and although neither of us could admit to being overawed by the sight of a bunch of seals flopped out on the sand, we had a pleasant enough few hours there. We had far more enjoyment from another of the Bradys' recommendations that evening when we ate at a restaurant run by an expatriate Czechoslovakian ('René's Place – Old World Cooking – Gourmet Food') on Lincoln City's main street. This was the best meal we had partaken of in living memory – Halibut in caper-and-portwine sauce, and Prawn Provençale. It cost us altogether less than thirty bucks and there wasn't the slightest trace of cinnamon in either dish.

Our stay at Lincoln City was entirely undramatic. We read, we wrote, and we hung out on various beautiful and quiet beaches, particularly at Pacific City, a tiny, funky little township some fifteen miles north of our base. There were no remarkable encounters. There were few holidaymakers now we were in mid-September. Driving back to the motel in the dark, deer would wait politely in the middle of the highway before trotting the rest of the way across once we'd passed. It was time out from the Great American Museum. But, as if stubbornly reminding us of exactly where things were at, as if to insist that I play the role of snotty, patronizing Brit, there was this sign outside a block of offices at Pacific City which were the premises of a dentist, a lawyer, an accountant and a realtor: it was a large, carefully painted board listing the names of the practitioners; and above these names was the title of the building. It read PROFFESIONAL SERVICES PLAZA.

6. *Nostalgie de la Frontière*

It was the day of the feast of Yom Kippur when we finally pulled out of Lincoln City and chugged off south on 101 towards the California line, and as we wended our way down the rocky coastline of south Oregon I duly gave myself the spiritual whipping for having had such a snide reaction to that simple matter of mis-spelling. After all, 'professional' was a word I'd buggered up myself on countless occasions (so was 'occasion' for that matter); and what did it matter anyway? Language was for-ever changing, and I didn't really care whether the word in question had two 'f's, or if 'colour' lost its 'u' or 'programme' dropped its final 'me'. So long as the thing communicated, that was all that mattered. Thus did I atone for the sin of condescension; but despite this, I still felt that the sign was a telling one. And there *is* a difference between a nite spot and a long dark nite of the soul, and I was sure most Americans would agree.

At Brookings near the California line all we could find was a forty-five-*Thaler* businessman's motel, but we took the opportunity to watch the HBO there: the movie was *Flatliners* with Kiefer Sutherland and Julia Roberts. The scenario was fine – a bunch of medical students decide to stop their hearts and go brain-dead for a few minutes and see what happens before bringing themselves round again. So then, what is the death experience about? The movie spelt it out loud and clear: what you first confront in those initial minutes is childhood guilt, pure and simple. Med student 1 had bullied one of his schoolmates; student 2 had videotaped makeouts with his lovers without their knowing; student 3 had tormented a black girl at junior school; and student 4 had had her father blow his brains out because she had accidentally witnessed him shooting up heroin. And what was to be done? Why, they had to expiate their sins by going and apologizing to those concerned. Once they have all done this, everything's OK, and the final frame shows a white-bearded God beaming down on them with satisfaction. And in case the message isn't clear enough, towards the end one of the kids says to the others, 'I guess what this is all about is *atonement*, right?' Well, sure, but atonement *after* death appears to me to be a little late in the day; moreover, to label the taping of sex and the witnessing of drug-taking as sins on a par with bullying and racism was just too ludicrous. But it made sense nevertheless: if America had the guts to look either of the first two phenomena straight in the face and legalize them both (because sex is more or less an illegal act, just as most of the narcotics trade is), it surely could kiss goodbye to all that repression-related crime and pain and wasted lives, and waste-of-time dramas based on the love-lives of preachers and politicians.

Early next morning we reached the state line, where we were stopped at the agricultural station's checkpoint and inspected for any infected apples we might be attempting to import. Since we had, appropriately, only a lime, we were waved through, and were immediately confronted with two California clichés: fruit-pickers in the fields and Fleetwood Mac on the radio. But for the next couple of days the golden state of popular imagination was distinctly absent. We followed 101 down the rocky, misty, autumnal and peculiarly English-looking coastline, passing through the sleazy old port-towns of Crescent City and Eureka. At Fort Bragg, in a funky little Mexican café down by the harbour we picked up a copy of a local newspaper: a sixteen-page broadsheet freebie called the *Mendocino Commentary*. A commentary paper was exactly what it was – no real news reporting, instead a collection of columns and editorials indicating that hereabouts in northern California was at least some kind of radical community. 'Publisher's corner' dealt with an incident that had taken place some weeks back in Ohio, when a drunk driver had wiped out a horse-drawn-buggy-load of Amish, killing six of them. The perpetrator was being charged merely with 'aggravated vehicular assault', and the column concluded:

The Amish are special people in our country, they embody innocence.

They don't believe in insurance and will not even consider suing anyone. Lawsuits are against their beliefs. A fund has been set up for the survivors. Why not help them now?

Other excerpts from the *Commentary* were as follows:

The country, like our city, our state, and our nation, is broke.

Ninety-nine per cent of us had sick and neurotic parents, even if we don't now realize it.

People For a Nuclear-Free Future would like to thank all those who helped to make Chicken Bingo a resounding success.

Our state has decided to charge us for going to our beaches – on this much we can agree: left, right and center we will fight like junkyard dogs. *Free Beaches For Free People.*

Terminator 2 was great – lots of big old Detroit cars blown to pieces and a Chevy Pickup shown to be an underpowered piece of sewage – and come to think of it, I'm going to get *rid* of my GMC product – it's got bumpers and lights and a bunch of crap features no one wants – computerized this and that – when what I want is a buggy to pull a cord of firewood up the hill and can be fixed with a screwdriver and plyers ...

From the 'Be Safe not Sorry' column:

Most head injuries in children are caused by shopping cart accidents. Never let a child 'ride' or 'skate' on a shopping cart ... A safe and sane birthday present: tattoo emergency phone numbers on out-of-the-way areas of your child's body such as the soles of the feet or an armpit. The first time a number is needed, the procedure pays for itself ... No normal child or adult 'likes to be alone'. Schizophrenia runs in families. Check your family history for suspicious incidents, and never be ashamed to turn yourself in. New therapies, treatments and surgical procedures are discovered every day.

From the 'Radio Free Earth' column:

A third of the kids graduated from American high schools last year are functionally illiterate. Nine out of ten high school graduates from America's class of '81 have read no more than one book per year since – and which books? Books stocked at Safeway: *A Desire too Hot,*

Brooding Wagons, Forbidden Apache Lust, ... coffee table books, *Garfield* books, diet books ...

Don't let anyone call you an antisemite because you don't want your pockets picked by Zionists. Don't be told you must pay to have Jews steal Palestinian land because Hitler was a bad guy.

Time to relate to children, families and friends is fast disappearing. Most parents in America are either neglecting or abusing their children while they struggle with a daily feeling of drowning. Welfare and school budgets are cut and legislators vote to double their pay. Old retired rich people play golf while the people who keep the greens in shape suffer homelessness and malnutrition. CNN, CBS, NBC and ABC etc. tell us every day 'Things are getting better.' Just how stupid are we? Just how big a lie are we willing to believe?

And from the phone-in classifieds:

A friend and I are doing a collage and we need cancelled food stamps – the yellow ones with tulips on them? Emily, PO Box 9308, Oregon 97370. Thanks. Peace.

The *Mendocino Commentary* was the voice of a generation come of age some twenty to thirty years ago but still not entirely seduced by the nation's consensus. Granted they had seen fit to print a large photo of a cute little kitten on their front page, but at least it wasn't a ribboned duck, and at least the paper wasn't *Rolling Stone*. There were obviously still some nonconformists alive and well in these parts. To find some more traces of them we drove seventy miles inland over the coastal range the next day to Ukiah, a town longer than it was wide, situated in the valley of the Russian River. Now we were away from the coastal fog, the Californian light was remarkable. It was like stepping into an early Technicolor movie, with its shimmering and almost unnatural intensity, especially when beholding the ring of surrounding mountains which were a glowing brown against a cloudless, vivid sky the colour of Doris Day's eyes. This dominant sandstone-umber and sky-blue is impossible to escape in California, and combines somehow to produce a light which is the colour of roasted peanuts and saturates every object.

Having checked into a motel on the outskirts of Ukiah (a quiet, lawned and tree-shaded place whose proprietors, originally from Vermont, were planning on moving to Oregon for 'more public beaches' as they put it), we re-checked an ad in the *Commentary:* 'Ukiah Playhouse. Glengarry Glen Ross, Th–Sat Thru 9–28 Ukiah Players Theater $7 "profane language" 462–9226.' This was a recent, highly rated play about real estate sharks in eighties' America, and we decided to see it that evening. We picked tickets up from a bookshop in the old downtown, the kind of place which sold the latest Pynchon and Martin Amis and had a large children's section complete with beanbags, and where at the checkout a couple of teachers were complaining to the salesgirl about the dire straits of their education budget. Later on we drove to the playhouse, which was a modest, recently constructed barn-like affair. Those who had come to fill its two hundred steeply raked seats and eat carrot cake and drink coffee or fruit juice in the foyer bore every resemblance to a British fringe theatre crowd except that they dressed a touch more formally, and were far more generous with their applause during the show – it seemed to be the convention in these parts to clap out a round after every crossfade and blackout, not just after each scene. In this way the theatre resembled more a TV studio, and it was easy to imagine that this pattern of a show constantly punctuated by ritual applause had been inherited from TV-land.

American cinema audiences also tend to be less passive than their British counterparts, as the gasps of horror, cries of encouragement and cheers of support demonstrated at the Ukiah cinema the following evening where we watched *Boyz in the Hood* and had ourselves a frighteningly vicarious experience of the processes by which the black dwellers of central LA are incited to forget about education and self-improvement and instead to depend on crack and guns and blow each other away in a twisted version of genocide. The internecine warfare of *Boyz,* invisibly encouraged by dominant white culture, was just a more extreme version of the kind of everyday squabbles that Larry Keith found himself sorting out down in South Carolina. It was yet one more insight into the depressing state of US education: blacks struggling to preserve their self-esteem against a white consensus promoting the idea that they were intellectually inferior by virtue of race. The one protagonist with enough belief in himself pulls through and gets out of the quagmire and away to college, but he sees too many of his friends settle for being merely streetwise, which only gets them killed in the end.

Of course it is in the interests of the powers that would like to continue ruling America to keep those whom they rule in such self-destructive ignorance. The day after seeing *Boyz* this fact was emphasized by a commercial on afternoon TV which was far more upfront than any Republican political broadcast would dare to be: an eighteen-year-old, over-coiffured, blond, blue-eyed, shirt'n'tie'd male spoke to camera, and this is what he said:

'Why go to college? I sent $250 for this fabulous, learn-at-home, six-month course in business administration, and I got a job within weeks of finishing. Why waste years of your life at college? You can have what every American wants – a car, a home and a family – and you can have it while you're still young – like me!'

There then followed details of the fabulous course which ensured that in six months' time you'd be a real *proffesional*.

It was at this stage of the trip, during that three-night stay in Ukiah, that a slightly sinister vision began to dominate my perceptions of the country. I began to feel completely overwhelmed by the Germanness of it all. It was not a matter of any serious comparison with the present-day Federal Republic of Germany; it was rather an accumulation of impressions, of language and habits, all of which were combining to make me feel I was visiting a kind of Neo-Germany, a country which bore more than a passing resemblance to the Deutschland of the 1930s. Perhaps it was an accident of the particular route we had taken: after all, there were nine states in the union which contained a town called Berlin, and we'd been through seven of them. But there was more to it than this. Roger Daniels, in his book about immigration, *Coming to America,* has said that 'The cultural apparatus created in the US by Germans in the nineteenth and early twentieth century dwarfs that of any other ethnic group.' And this hegemony was beginning to pop out at me from everywhere I looked. What was I seeing? Fat people in droves with a fondness for hot dogs, Hamburgers, and beer by Budweiser, Coors, Michelob, Becks and Schlitz; folk in squarehead caps driving along autobahns through pine-covered hills, exchanging

Thalers for goods. I was seeing every derogatory cliché of the porked-out Kraut alive and well in the USA; but what had it to do with the thirties in particular? Everything, it seemed: Bauhaus typography, flag-waving nationalism, and that great obsession with body-culture and sport, particularly baseball and football, which fell only marginally short of being military activities. What was it Frank had told us in Chugwater? He had said that the sport thing was taking over in schools at the expense of intellectual education, and that if a teacher went looking for a job his or her employers were primarily interested in the sports he or she could coach. It wasn't good enough to be an excellent Math or English teacher – if you couldn't coach at least two sports you had little chance against your rival applicants. Sports, parades, marching bands, flags, encouragement of mass-conformity, degradation of the intellect, ghettos, stacked courts, political control of the reproductive process – all these things had been hallmarks of the old Third Reich, and they were running rampant in the USA today. Not to mention the saccharescent sentiment and the overbearing cuteness which is always the flip side of a brutal nature, and of callous murders and symbolic eagles. Yes – and was not the gas chamber also alive and functioning in this country? And wasn't the old *Kinder-Küche-Kirche* sorority – which is of course the ladies' branch of the Ku-Klux-Klan – still being heavily promoted? And where was the political resistance? Not in Congress. There, the Democrats and Republicans looked more than ever like two wings of the same party. The only voices of dissent were coming from isolated individuals like Frank; the black-and-therefore-deemed-unelectable politician Jesse Jackson; and the frustrated sixties' children of northern California without a cent to rub between them for any serious political campaigning. It was looking less and less likely that anyone would get up in 1992 and make a real stand against a political mafia who for a generation had been crushing blacks, women, workers, gays, intellectuals, and every other category of folk whom Hitler had once blessed with their very own personalized badge of contempt, be the triangles pink, yellow, red or polka-dot. Schools-to-prisons; New Order; ancient myths; stacked courts and censored thoughts; grand pretentious architectures alongside disease-ridden ghettos; a population that if not disabled by heinous narcotic cocktails was junked up with terrible overdoses of bronze-age religion and rock music. For Wagner substitute stadium rock; for Nuremburg substitute the World Series football; for a media and a political establishment controlled by the military-industrial complex, no substitute necessary; in America now as Germany then; for *Lebensraum* – since the USA already has plenty of 'raum' to 'leben' in – substitute periodic overseas military adventures, plus SDI, plus what was left of global economic domination. Ironically, the Jews, especially the Zionists, weren't particularly suffering this time around, in fact they had US Mid-East policy by the balls; no – for Jews, substitute blacks; for Führer substitute Jehovah; and finally, for that brief period of the flowering of enlightened ideas which took place in the Germany of the twenties, substitute the sixties and mythologize it as a ghastly childish aberrance, and place its protagonists into the bland angst of a TV ghetto like *Thirtysomething,* in which those one-time rebellious children can wear their hair long provided they buy into the great American *Traum* of car-family-kids and a degree in business studies. And if they still complain, why just audit them every year.

Gott-in-Himmel, was it really this gruesome? Yes, of course it was. Greater minds than mine had already been describing the parts of this sum for years. Vidal sat in Italy, sending out periodic dispatches; Stone was busy making a movie about the Kennedy assassination conspiracy; Burroughs sat 'quietly in the future' in Lawrence, Kansas, elegantly satirizing the whole tamale. Dylan, Ferlinghetti, Ginsberg *et al.* had been shouting about it for decades from the enlightened outposts of New York and San Francisco. The Fourth Reich was rolling on, meat-hatted, heavily armed and pickup-trucked, back to the future of mad monotheistic middle-eastern prophets stoned on desert roots, blood and iron, celibate anger and dreams of an impossibly pure paradise that would compensate them for the sheer hell of a life that had been a torment ever since they had been pulled prematurely from the tit and slapped around the head from the first time their hands had strayed towards those personal zones of earthly pleasure. White men as frustrated as any dispossessed Palestinian regularly crashed into restaurants and gunned down those inside; while the majority, whose passions had not quite boiled over, walked around with fixed smiles on their faces, spraying strangers with bursts of automatic politesse, the men bound by muscles, the women by image.

As we travelled out of Ukiah and down 101 towards San Francisco I counted the U-Hauls moving steadfastly in the other direction. Urban California's problems – economic, environmental, social – were well documented by now, but what was being done about them, where were the political initiatives? The only such project I could discover was documented in a Marin County newspaper: somebody was starting a campaign (later to enjoy some legislative success) to outlaw the wearing of strong perfumes in public places such as restaurants, buses and trains. Now here was the kind of political will the country needed to jump-start it back into health.

Since we were driving straight through San Francisco for now, we stuck to the elevated freeway; but soon discovered that a large section in the south of the city was still closed – a result of the earthquake of two years ago. Not that it had collapsed like the Nimitz over in Oakland – but it was constructed in the same manner and so was not to be trusted. Not that any redesigning or reinforcing project was under way, either; perhaps there was just no cash for it. Whatever, as we found out some days later, it meant traffic in peak hours was forced to take a tortuous route round and about the streets below, thereby exaggerating the normal gridlock conditions. But now as we wound our way through the city we admired the pastel shades of its housing, and the rather beautiful way in which the fog patches are so strictly demarcated: these nebulous masses overhang the hillsides and roads like floating cigar-shaped UFOs. The cool, dappled landscape quickly disappeared as we left the city and headed over the Santa Cruz mountains through yet more of those interminable redwood forests that had plagued the route since our first entrance to the state and which I haven't mentioned up till now for the sake of decency. Redwoods: forests of them; avenues-of-giant-redwoods; drive-thru redwoods. And every single tree seemed to hold an irresistible attraction for that other plague of the California highways, the old folk in their cream-and-tan RVs, often with a car in tow, often with a smaller RV in tow, complete with air-conditioning, TV and little yappy dog, using up enough energy resources in half an hour to keep a Third World country going for half a year; and their motoring holidays seemed to have the sole purpose of being able to return and say 'We saw every single tree in California – and here's the photos to prove it.' Yep. Used up a whole rain forest to make that trip. Passing denizens of these vehicles parked up in lines at sunset on some lot overlooking the Pacific, it appeared as if all these folks had made their way west until there was no further they could go, and now they were just staring out to the sea in the vain hope that sooner or later, by divine ordinance, a great highway would rise magically and majestically from the waves, lined with redwoods, punctuated by state parks (i.e. a grassy clearing with a wooden picnic table and BBQ grill), and lead them away beyond the final frontier to the West beyond the West, to the New Jerusalem, to the Happy Camping Grounds where gas was cheap, steaks were thick, Eisenhower was in the White House and *Mr Ed* was on TV. In a sense all of America was afflicted by this *nostalgie de la frontière*, waiting for the next leap forward, the next big idea. So far they were waiting in vain. 'Watch California,' said *Time* magazine. 'Whatever happens there happens to America before long and to the entire world a little after that.' The future happens first in California? I don't think so, not anymore. All they are claiming now are the 'innovations' of racial and ethnic tensions, overcrowding, declining industry and ecological disaster. Wonderful as the Great American Drive-thru Museum was, the 'future exhibits' section appeared to be empty.

Peter and Leah Korchien were still investing, however. We arrived at their spacious one-storey house in the suburbs of Santa Cruz to find it in the final stages of a rebuilding programme, with builders' rubble outside and bare concrete floors inside. The Korchiens were friends of Rosey's parents – Peter was a scientist who worked for Lockheed, enthusiastic, eggheaded, bespectacled; Leah taught baroque music at the nearby university; and their sixteen-year-old daughter Deborah, who bore a startling resemblance to Robert de Niro, was supposed to be something of a keyboard prodigy. Our first words to the Korchiens were 'Do you know anyone who wants to buy our car?' – since by now we were only days away from departing the country. And, to our surprise, it turned out that they were at this moment looking for a 'cheap car' for Deborah's birthday present. Peter immediately test-drove the Datsun, taking me with him on a tour of the university campus; he pointed out various buildings that were apparently there hiding behind the pine trees in the pitch dark of the evening. Since I couldn't see the buildings in question, Peter gave me a glowing description of their architecture, to which I responded enthusiastically. So this was Virtual Reality. Anyway, Peter liked the car and was prepared to buy it from us; Deborah, on the other hand, who was consulted when we returned, pulled the kind of face that suggested she'd been asked to accept a can of dogshit. It turned out that while we'd been out, a friend had telephoned and offered his car to her. According to Leah it was a snip at three thousand bucks.

'Aaron Levinson's Mustang?' said Peter. 'I heard it was a grief car.'

Perhaps, but it was a Ford Mustang, nineteen sixty-five, as Wilson Pickett used to sing. Somehow 'Datsun Sally' didn't quite make it as an alternative title. It was obvious that Deborah wouldn't be seen dead in our old wreck, and that with her mother's support she would prevail. Just as with Hazel's van up in Lincoln City, it was a case of My Country's Car, right or wrong, and to hell with the bills.

After this, Deborah was allowed to go out socializing for the night provided she promise to do three extra hours' piano practice the next day; this promise having been eventually extracted from her, she disappeared and left the four of us to dinner, during which we were treated to the full story of the house's conversion, complete with architectural blueprints and a thousand action shots of Peter and others in plaster-besmeared jeans, clutching various power tools. After dinner there was no let-up in our crash course in local education: the earthquake album was fetched out and we were talked through it at length.

California is big on Acts of God, be it forest fire, flood or earthquake; perhaps this is because so many places are named after His saints. Saint Andrew in particular is blamed for every seismographic disturbance, and he honoured Santa Cruz two years back by choosing it as the epicentre of the 'quake. When we visited the downtown area the next day we were startled, not so much by the visible devastation of a town centre ravaged by a cluster of huge craters and cracked, crazy streets, and temporary marquee-like trading centres everywhere – but by the fact that there had yet to begin any rebuilding process. Like the weed-cracked empty freeways of San Francisco, the desolation remained; nobody was reinvesting. The only signs of optimism in downtown Santa Cruz were amongst the crowds of young people begging on the streets, chatting happily amongst themselves as they revelled in the recent news that a court case had now effectively legalized panhandling in the state, and they could now ask for spare change without risking a night in jail. But the interesting angle on this event was that the case – fought by an unemployed San Franciscan bus driver – had hinged upon the man's appeal to the First Amendment guarantee of freedom of speech; in other words, this heroic mendicant had forced the richest state in the union finally to allow someone to stand up in public and proclaim he or she was broke, and then to suggest that any passer-by might care to help redress the situation. Thus a long-lasting taboo on the mere mention of poverty here in the golden state of opportunity had been broken: Californians were now allowed to admit they had no money. Now this really did seem like something new under the sunshine.

After a couple of nights at the contradictory Korchiens, who didn't seem to have a care in the world, bar one or two peremptory and ritual serious remarks about the recession, we set off again for San Francisco where on Columbus Avenue I stepped through the hallowed portals of the City Lights bookstore. It wasn't such a romantic experience: it resembled Compendium in Camden Town, only it was smaller, and it stocked far less beat-genre titles than were available in the London shop. Even the copy of Burroughs' *The Western Lands* that I purchased bore the outlandishly regular imprint of Penguin Books. But I was happy to support the dear old gent – a book of his essays had sustained me during all those many motel stop-overs when an antidote had been required to counteract the endless stream of drug-crazed, paranoid hallucinations I was coming across each night in the pages of my Gideon Bible. One day, if I should ever become rich, I will take a leaf out of Bernard Coffindaffer's book and make a pilgrimage across the nation; and in every hotel and motel room across the land, from Frostproof, Florida, to Mechanic Falls, Maine, to Walla Walla, Washington, to Cardiff-by-the-Sea, California; in Turkey, Texas; Arab, Alabama; Mikado, Michigan; Midnight, Mississippi; New Babylon, New

York; Paint, Pennsylvania; Vesuvius, Virginia; Climax, Colorado; and Omega, Ohio – I will assiduously place, beside a copy of every Bible, a volume of Bill Burroughs' collected works; and may their pages intertwine in the dark of the night, and breed strange literary mutants that will take off through an open window, and flap darkly across the moon, and fly into the dreams of sleeping Americans everywhere: they might run themselves up the flagpole, and replace Old Glory with the Great American Ribboned Duck; they might place the smiling head of Martin Luther King Jr into every basketball net of every citizen's front yard; they might cause every satellite dish to beam out concentrated, endless waves of orgone energy that will abolish the fear of reproductive processes for ever; then again, they might just all get shot down by every citizen's private arsenal of handguns, shotguns and night-seeing semi-automatics: 'Never could stand a mutant. Praise the Lord and pass the remote.'

Twenty years ago the Haight-Ashbury district of San Francisco, up on the hill just south of the Golden Gate park panhandle, was world famous as the epicentre of a city supposed to be itself the focal point of a great countercultural movement. The baby-boomers were coming of age, tuning in, turning on and (briefly at least) dropping out, which often meant hanging out in Haight-Ashbury. As the era wound down and the troops came home from Asia, Haight-Ashbury gained itself a more unsavoury reputation as the home of hippy leftovers too whacked-out to move on, of decaying housing, street crime and smack culture, backdated, symbolic of a dream that had died. These days the wide streets with their tall, four-storey brick houses built some hundred years ago, are slowly being gentrified, and those who throng Haight Street, the main drag which sells mainly books, clothing and records, are a mixture of the middle-class and the street-class, spiced with a flavoursome assortment of bums, junkies, winos, panhandlers and lunatics. And it's still a youth culture here, whatever your income. However, it feels derivative rather than avant-garde; it's like Camden Lock, London, with everything but the market stalls, and it appears to take its cultural cues from London youth, whose music and attitude has perhaps been lent more of a cutting edge in recent years simply by being exposed for much longer to the downside of a decade of monetarism, recession and intolerance. There's certainly little that feels intrinsically American about this neighbourhood – unless you count the ridiculous price of cigarette papers (a dollar a packet): this particular phenomenon is a direct result of the 'war on drugs', whose puny logic assumes that if you make Rizlas expensive, then folk will instantly cease to roll up marijuana, heroin and everything else in them, and the problem will be solved, as sure as death in Texas. Cute, wasn't it?

We were here for practical rather than sentimental reasons. My old friend Susan Franklin lived just off Haight Street, and we were staying with her family for the last few days of our trip. Susan is from an upper-class Baltimore family, ex-debutante, ex-Bennington; and I first knew her twelve years ago when she was twenty years old and came over to study theatre at a rural art college in south-west England where I, too, was pursuing enlightenment. An insufferable snob when she first arrived (as she herself admits), four years at this institution had considerably shaken her up and opened her eyes. Not that the influences there had much to do with anything intrinsically British – the college had been co-founded by a member of the Whitney clan (of banking and art museum fame) and its performance course was heavily loaded with American teachers and the example of post-war American practitioners such as Charles Olson, John Cage, Merce Cunningham, Ed Dorn, Robert Wilson, Mary Caroline Richards, Susan Sontag, Anne Halprin and Richard Foreman. And through all its classes and workshops, students were thoroughly immersed in a wide catalogue of esoterica: bio-dynamics, encounter groups, mind-body-spirit, Zen Buddhism, shamanism, ritual catharsis, massage, Alexander Technique, crystal therapy, reflexology, Steinerism, Rajneeshism, Feminism, Paganism, witchcraft, psychoanalysis, alchemy, astrology, scientology, and so on *ad astra*. The college was a little corner of California, spiked with essence of SoHo, in the middle of South Devon. It had made me even more of a proxy American, and it made it entirely understandable that Susan Franklin would eventually settle in San Francisco, and now have a job selling homoeopathic medicines. I hadn't seen much of her since college days and was curious to see how she'd turned out. How Californian was she?

Extremely restless was one measure of it: looked at in terms of American history, when you've reached the West Coast and there's no more land to trek across (and if you're not happy just staring at the Pacific sunset from your motorized coffin of an RV), why, the only way forwards is upwards or inwards: is this why Californians have gained their reputation for cosmic wackiness coupled with psychological obsessions? Confronted with the physical barrier of the ocean, the final frontier is no longer topographical, but personal or astronomical; it makes of you a trekkie or a therapy-freak; it makes you do anything but stop moving.

Susan and husband Rob, together with three young children, live in the top half of a tall, rather narrow house reminiscent of the buildings in Amsterdam's old Jewish quarter; the stairways were steep and cramped but the rooms were large and high-ceilinged. Susan, a tall, dirty blonde, had plumped out since I had last seen her; she moved swiftly around the place like a speeded-up steamroller, giving out instructions and advice to all as she went, grabbing snacks and gulps from a glass of wine, answering the telephone, dealing swiftly with the sundry problems of each of the kids, reminding her husband of this duty or that task, hurrying up to her office under the roof, hurrying back, making calls, making sure that the wheels of her domain never stopped turning. It was an awesome example of dynamic matriarchy. Husband Rob, by way of complete contrast, was a soft-spoken man who moved slowly and quietly around in the midst of the turmoil. He wore floppy clothes, had large kindly eyes and unkempt curly hair, and appeared thoroughly self-effacing. There are plenty of San Franciscans, especially those associated with groups such as the notorious Men, Sex and Power, who would have summed Rob up with a simple idiom: 'pussy-whipped', they would surely have called him, and suggested he come along to their sessions, jump up and down, roar, beat his chest and generally come on like a furious mandrill, and thus rid himself of the destructive effeteness that years of fascistic feminism had beaten into the once-great US male. I don't think Rob had any of this kind of problem, and he certainly didn't need any of the kind of male-reassertion treatments which were basically borne of military nostalgia. It's just that he and his wife were an oddly contrasting couple, and it was clear that much of Susan's restlessness stemmed from marital frustrations.

Our arrival on the scene had also stirred her up in anticipation of the solo trip to England she would shortly be making, back to her old haunts, back to her old friends, some of whom she hadn't seen for a decade. The evening after our arrival we sat on the back porch in the cool night air, drinking wine and smoking cigarettes, and talking of those friends. Rob and kids had gone to bed.

'How's Jim?' asked Susan. Jim was a mutual friend with whom a decade ago she had enjoyed a brief affair, suddenly ended when Susan had had to scurry off home for a family funeral from which she didn't return till after her marriage. It was a scrappy affair even while it lasted, shot through as it was with mutual infidelities. So I told her how Jim was – restless, dissatisfied, as it happened.

'Mmm,' said Susan. 'You know, I've got some unfinished business with him?' The more we talked about England, the more it was clear that Susan missed it terribly – the Devon countryside, her old black Morris Minor, the climate, the theatre, her old girlfriends. But as more and more old men friends came up for discussion, it became clear that Susan was fully intending to fuck her way across the country for four weeks of untrammelled bliss.

Not that she was particularly trammelled at the moment: the next day she raced us out in her Chevy van for a tour of the Napa Valley wineries, and as we sat on the terrace of a newly built French château, nibbling canapés of caviar and sipping champagne, Susan happily confessed that she was currently running an affair with her tennis partner, and it was by no means the first.

Well, excuse us, Susan, but why did you ever get married, and why Rob?

'Oh,' said Susan, the sun glinting on her Raybans, 'Rob's like a warm slipper ...'

Through the vineyards of the Napa Valley we whizzed, snacking and drinking as we went from fake château to pseudo-hacienda, to Japanese sake factory complete with Zen garden of rocks and raked sand. Another virtual-reality land of postmodern simulacra. And as we went, by way of strange counterpoint to the theme of Susan's dominant rampages through the vineyards of male sexuality, she related to us the story of a woman friend who had been slavishly bound to an apparent tyrant of a man, constantly leaving him only to return to be further mistreated; she would complain to him how miserable he was making her, we were told, and he in turn would say, 'Well why don't you kill yourself? I know you will sooner or later.' And a year ago to this day, Susan told us, she had come out here to the valley, lain down in a vineyard, taken off her blouse and skirt, folded them neatly some feet away, and then put a bullet through her head.

Another glass of Cabernet Sauve-qui-peut? Cheers.

I'm in no position to analyse or give judgement on the marriage of Susan and Rob. I could say by way of indicator that all three of the pretty blonde kids seemed to carry in them a certain underlying anxiety, but how much can you really ascertain in three days? I could say that Susan's husband was a happy man who enjoyed being a victim, or a manipulated fool, or someone who was for now putting up quietly with the shit but who would sooner or later protest and assert himself. One afternoon we witnessed Rob come in with a selection of different locks and catches for the back porch door: Susan sat at the kitchen table while he held up each lock in its proposed position, and she gave her preferences and comments in a manner that suggested her husband was some dickheaded tradesman; he put up with her brusque and peremptory manner quite remarkably. Perhaps this dynamic was something the pair of them had worked out between themselves, with no undue problems attached; but I doubted it. Susan was just too raunchy, too restless, too concerned with a life that didn't have much room for husband and children. I think she was looking forward to a time when the kids would be grown up and she could wash her hands of it all. Not that the kids didn't spend most of the time supervised by the young English nanny from 'Nottinill'.

Rob had at least one interest in the future: he was a *Star Trek II* fan, and I watched an episode with him one evening. Would there be any telling, Barthesian clues to the state of the nation from this show? What was happening on the final frontier? Well – the captain of the Enterprise was no longer American, but a fruity-voiced bald-headed Brit, no less; while the American fellow on board turned out not to be a man at all, but a robot. *Interprète-qui-ôse.*

Meanwhile we still had to sell our car. After we'd placed ads on the lamp posts along Haight Street for the weekend crowds, a couple of El Salvadoreans – a woman and her husband, whose name was Jesus – came by, test-drove it round the block, and were instantly willing to give us three hundred dollars for it. There was only one problem: we didn't yet have the title certificate. America controls the sale of motor vehicles with as much vehemence as it regulates its reproductive activities and, just as when we'd bought the car back in South Carolina, the complete bureaucratic palava was required – the exchange of vehicle for cash, handshake and scribbled receipt wasn't enough. We'd left South Carolina too quickly for the authorities to draw up a title in our name, and we were now waiting for it to arrive by post courtesy of Ffarington, who had sent it off by express mail more than two weeks ago. It still hadn't arrived. Maybe tomorrow? Tomorrow came, and so did Jesus and a pal of his, but still there was no title. It wasn't snow or rain or heat or gloom staying the couriers of the US Mail, just their notorious ineptitude. Still hoping there might be a way around the problem, the four of us drove over to the local Department of Motor Vehicles. Sorry, they said – no title, no sale. We trudged dejectedly out of the office. But then Jesus had a rapid consultation with his mate and offered us $100 for the Datsun – it looked like he would do a little underhand transferring of documents and plates from another, smashed-up Datsun he had or would obtain, and thus circumvent the problem. So we cleared the 210 of six thousand miles' worth of accumulated junk, maps and radio, and then followed Jesus across town, into a scruffy backstreet and thence to a lot littered with wrecks, dogs, and toddling children. There we bade our chariot farewell, and Jesus handed us the cash before giving us a lift back to Haight Street. We couldn't complain – we'd had more than our money's worth out of that car. Nevertheless, we were then besieged with sympathetic outrage and advice from all and sundry, all of whom advised us immediately to sue the US Mail for the money we'd lost on the deal, and some; and it took us a while to quell their savage litigatory urges and convince Susan, Rob and friends that it just wasn't worth it. Soothing the American rage to complain was quite a job. I had the feeling that before very long we'd be hearing of citizens suing their government for the recession, or taking their ageing parents to court to accuse them of having been dysfunctional and thereby violating their children's civil rights under various articles of the Constitution. This urge for redress and recompense is just one more way in which attention is focused squarely on the past, on incidents and injustices real or imagined. When this gets out of hand, as it often does in America, it produces individuals who dedicate their whole lives to fighting complex and everlasting cases, like the gentleman who has been suing a medical company because they used a body cell of his – obtained during the course of medical treatment and without his knowledge – to pioneer a profitable new way of fighting disease. He says he wants justice – but justice in so many cases has merely become a synonym for money.

The study of the past – of history – can be a healthy enterprise. But when this activity becomes obsessively subjective or profit-based it begins to lose its value, and the future starts to lose any meaning. There are countless examples of young (and not-so-young) Americans obsessed with the 'sins' of their parents and their own childhood traumas, just like Ed and Jenny Bauer; and this hyper-Freudianism was echoed in Susan Franklin's definition of her own homoeopathic practice: for her, the discipline was about isolating the significant 'miasm' or childhood trauma in the patient's history, and then prescribing the appropriate drug. For instance, I myself suffer periodically from headaches, and Susan decided to cure me, despite my protestations that they were probably caused either by too much alcohol or by too much thinking. No – my headaches were due to some childhood trauma that had remained unpurged. Could I remember any such incidents from my past? Well, yes, there were plenty, caused by my own stupidity, or arrogance or by mere bad luck; but none of these would do for Susan. She was looking for something caused by my parents – had they beaten me, perhaps, or left me ever? So I mentioned that my father had left when I was seven; I added that I had been a lot happier since he had done so, but this fact was conveniently dealt with – I was told that it had indeed made me unhappy, it was just that I'd suppressed these feelings. Susan was triumphant. She had found her miasm and she had found the appropriate perpetrator. I was duly prescribed the appropriate drug. I still get a headache when I think about all this.

Within twenty-four hours of selling the car, we flew out of San Francisco en route to Sydney, Australia. Another day, another town. But even after the brief stop-over at Honolulu, we were still not out of the USA. We were flying United Airlines, which meant an all-American environment right across the Pacific. So up in front of us on the big screen was projected a non-stop diet of US news and sport, with the same programme constantly repeated every couple of hours; so that every time I looked up from my Burroughs, there was the same little-league baseball match – one that I got to know in detail. A team of nordic-looking kids from Wisconsin was playing a side from the West Coast consisting entirely of East Asians, Sino-Japanese types. There on the screen were all the square caps and leather accoutrements. This was my last chance to discover the missing element that I had been sensing throughout the whole of the trip, but had been unable to put my finger on: what was it that made this game such a Teutonic museum-piece? The pitchers wound up and threw; the batters swiped and ran; the outfielders pursued the ball with their giant, mutant hand ... then I had it. It was the knickerbockers! The same item of archaic central-European clothing sometimes to be seen in North London on a Saturday sported by the boy children of Hasidic Jews along with their square caps and old-fashioned tight-fitting flared jackets; an item of unmitigated nostalgia – only in this case it wasn't being worn by a few members of a minority religious sect, but by hundreds of thousands of American sportsmen – baseball players *and* footballers, every day of the week. This was an American costume-dream that harked back to the great days of American expansion: to Teddy Roosevelt, to the explosion of industry and invention, to the rising of the skyscrapers, to the influx of the huddled masses, the millions of immigrants – above all in that era the Germans, teeming in through Ellis Island, spreading across the states, into the cities and the countryside alike, building their Berlins, their breweries, their ball-bearing factories, their churches, synagogues, schools, farms and dance-halls, their theatres and film studios, shops, law firms, universities and publishing houses. And most of them were not coming to escape some vile trauma in the land of their birth; they came rather with a solid vision – plan might be more accurate – of the future.

As the knickerbockers scuttled round the baseball field, the screen seemed to flicker and turn monochrome for an instant. All the glories of the past subtly implied in a pair of knee-length pants visible on every TV screen, every day of the American year.

An hour out from Sydney the game showed for the last time. The white kids were losing badly to their shorter, darker-skinned opponents. As the West Coast team hit a home run, one more German connection occurred to me:

Sigmund Freud was another highly significant US import from German-speaking Europe. It was after this man's initial trip to the States in 1909 that his theories began to catch on in the wider world; and it was in the US more than anywhere that the movement blossomed. As is well known, Freudian therapeutics is an essentially pessimistic affair. It concentrates ruthlessly on the past, on sex and family. The future doesn't get much of a look in in the Freudian scheme of things. The man himself stated quite clearly that he could never claim to cure a patient, but merely make that person's life a little less miserable; and his coke-crazy works are shot through with a profoundly disenchanted view of the world. The biographies give the impression of Freud in old age as someone sitting in Nazi-occupied Vienna in 1938 in a state of extreme apathy, from where American Ambassador Bullitt had almost forcibly to extract him.

Now, it is arguable that by the end of the nineteenth century, with the West won and the nation complete, the US had entered its golden age of industrialism and invention; but this phase in turn begins to peter out by the end of World War II, and from now on, once the elements of the post-war world are in position – the automobile, highrise cities, electricity, jetplanes, TV, nuclear powers, Elvis, and psychoanalysis – from this point America begins to look back in earnest. Because apart from outer space, which entails far too great an imaginative leap for most, there is nowhere left to go. Except back to the Bible; and back to the analyst – time and time again.

America jumps in the car and drives its kids to what schools are left; then drives to the bank to take out what money is left, then spends it all on the church, the hospital, the therapist and the lawyer's fees, then watches back-to-back Back-To-The-Futures, or maybe *The Last Picture Show,* or perhaps even *JFK*, to catch a taste of that brief flowering of optimism so rudely snuffed out in the sixties. The upbeat of that age is symbolized by Kennedy, the 'counterculture' (usually an ecstatic topless dancer covered in bodypaint), the space programme, and the civil rights struggles. But then the future was assassinated along with JFK and King and Malcolm X; civil rights got bogged down in half-measures; the young died choking on their own vomit else in Vietnam else by their own National Guard, else they surrendered, or went into exile to end up bleating about the 'innocence' of the Amish from their north Californian hide-aways. The pessimists won – that's what a pessimist would say. But this is everyday America, the land of the Big Whinge, where we display our bleeding wounds in public, where we mourn and murmur and repine; 'tear-up' and whine and stamp our feet and demand retribution, and dribble angrily into the microphones of Oprah Winfrey and Phil Donohue: 'My parents sexually abused me! Freud was *wrong!* He *betrayed* me! Look, these are *real tears*! Where's my *money*?'

But more than one child survived, not least the interstate project: a new system of neural pathways expanding across the nation like the budding brains of a baby, to take at any speed and direction you like, and at very low cost. I think that's creative. My own dendrites devoured *Janet and John* at a formative stage and gave me an appetite for the USA, and that's why my guts turn over like a motor when I step on to its tarmac and smell dust, cinnamon and engine oil. I get a sense of infinite possibility pitted against fundamental stupidity, of mutation versus anachronism. And since mutants usually prevail, why not be optimistic? Why not drive a six-lane highway through a quiet backyard or across some sacred mountain or over some implausible pony or ribbonned duck? There's plenty more where those came from. Newcomers will crank up the moribund motels, new, live ghosts will appear. The châteaux in the Napa Valley will grow old and dignified. Coffindaffer clusters will rot where they stand and feed the crops, else change hands for millions of dollars. The '79 Toyota Coronet and the '78 Datsun 210 will become cultural icons. Narcotics will be decriminalized, but perfume will be prohibited, leading to a rash of scent-related crime. And Saxon America, minoritized and confined to reservations, will be forced by the threat of extinction to rediscover its long-erased genitals and body odours.

I directed this last prophecy towards the blond, blue-eyed pitcher in the strange old costume as he looked out, bewildered, from the screen: the peak of his meat hat had gone floppy, and he was sweaty and dishevelled; he'd just played his losing game for the fifth time, and was looking worse with every showing; all this repetition was getting him nowhere.

But America had the last word. It was 3 October, 1991, and back behind us on the mainland a certain middle-aged mutant babyboomer, a sax-playing, draft-dodging bookworm who just said yes-and-no to drugs and – no coincidence, this – was married to a shit-hot lawyer, was standing up to announce he was running for President. Now there's an all-American happy ending.